Presented to:

Mom

Presented by:

amy

Date:

12-25-03

E-MAIL FROM GOD
FOR WOMEN

by

Claire Cloninger

RIVER
OAK
PUBLISHING

Tulsa, Oklahoma

E-mail from God for Women
ISBN 1-58919-998-7
Copyright © 2001 by Claire Cloninger
Represented by: Alive Communications, Inc.
7680 Goddard Street
Suite 200
Colorado Springs, CO 80920

Published by RiverOak Publishing
P.O. Box 700143
Tulsa, OK 74170-0143

DEDICATION

This book is dedicated to my women friends,
a.k.a. "the holy steel magnolias."
You have strengthened my life with your prayer.
You have lightened my load with your laughter.
I love you!

INTRODUCTION

Since my sister Ann and her husband, Ed, moved to Kunming, China, two years ago, we've been amazed at the difference our e-mail "conversations" have made in keeping us close despite the miles that lie between us.

God has his own system of staying close to his children. He is constantly leaving messages in our spiritual e-mail boxes—messages that are current and personally relevant to the lives we lead as twenty-first century women.

Whether you're single or married, a professional woman or a stay-at-home mom, you've got mail in this book. Scripture-inspired love notes from God's heart to yours are found on every page. Set in the e-mail format, these are life-giving messages of hope, humor, compassion, courage, comfort, and practical advice from the Father to you, the daughter he loves.

So why wait? Log on to your Father's heart today!

DON'T LET YOUR ENEMY IN

Do not be anxious about anything, but in everything, by prayer and petition, with thanksgiving, present your requests to God. And the peace of God, which transcends all understanding, will guard your hearts and your minds in Christ Jesus.

Philippians | 4:6-7

Dear Child,

>Worry is an enemy that arrives on your doorstep disguised as a friend. When you're in trouble, Worry says, "Stick with me, kid. I'll help you deal with this." What a lie! Worry never contributes anything positive. It's a circular thought pattern that only leads to more worry, and in the end it leaves you with a knot in your stomach and no plan of action.

So when you hear the knock, knock, knock of worry at your door, don't answer. Instead, pray. Ask for my help. Trust me. Thank me. I'll lead you to my solution, and I'll station my peace like a guard outside your heart to keep worry off the premises.

Your Peace-giver,
>God

== == ==   == == == == == == == == ==

PEACE THAT DANCES

The fruit of the Spirit is . . .
joy [and] peace.

| Galatians | 5:22 |

Child of Mine,

>Someone once defined joy as "peace dancing." Can you relate to that? Unlike happiness, joy is not influenced by what's happening around you. It's an inner assurance that I am "the blessed controller of all things." It's a grateful realization that I treasure you with unbounded love that can never be taken from you.

When you are dwelling in joy, there will be no room for fear or depression. Your face will wear a new expression, and your heart will know a new serenity. I encourage you to cultivate this spiritual fruit of joy. Let your peace rise up in a joyful dance.

The Joy-giver,
>God

== == ==   == == == == == == == == ==

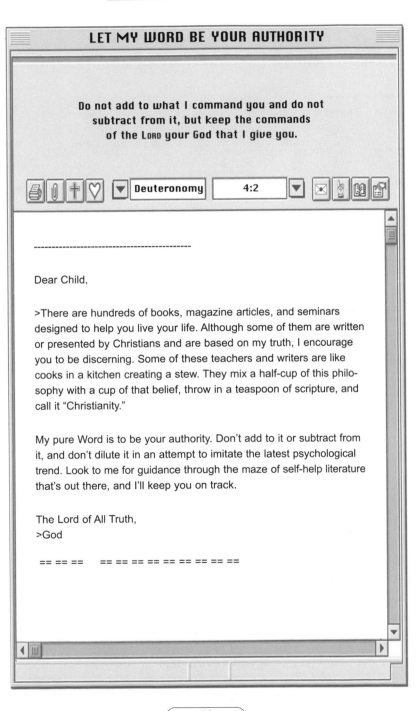

LET MY WORD BE YOUR AUTHORITY

Do not add to what I command you and do not subtract from it, but keep the commands of the LORD your God that I give you.

Deuteronomy 4:2

Dear Child,

>There are hundreds of books, magazine articles, and seminars designed to help you live your life. Although some of them are written or presented by Christians and are based on my truth, I encourage you to be discerning. Some of these teachers and writers are like cooks in a kitchen creating a stew. They mix a half-cup of this philosophy with a cup of that belief, throw in a teaspoon of scripture, and call it "Christianity."

My pure Word is to be your authority. Don't add to it or subtract from it, and don't dilute it in an attempt to imitate the latest psychological trend. Look to me for guidance through the maze of self-help literature that's out there, and I'll keep you on track.

The Lord of All Truth,
>God

== == ==   == == == == == == == == ==

WHAT'S PLAYING ON YOUR MIND?

Finally, brothers, whatever is true, whatever is noble,
whatever is right, whatever is pure, whatever is lovely,
whatever is admirable—if anything is excellent or
praiseworthy—think about such things.

Philippians   **4:8**

Dear Child,

>Your mind is a little bit like a movie theater that runs the films of your thoughts, your affections, and your values. If you could x-ray the minds of people passing by, you'd see a variety of movies. Some would center on a fresh excitement for the new day. Some would show the faces of loved ones. Some might even reveal a joyful mental dance of praise. But you'd see other kinds of mind-movies, too—the self-centered dreams of the greedy, the pornography and trash of a misguided culture.

What's playing on your mind today? If the themes of your movies have been envy, fear, or lust, confess and let me cleanse you. Then I'll turn on my movies of peace and joy.

The One Who Renews You,
>God

== == ==　 == == == == == == == == ==

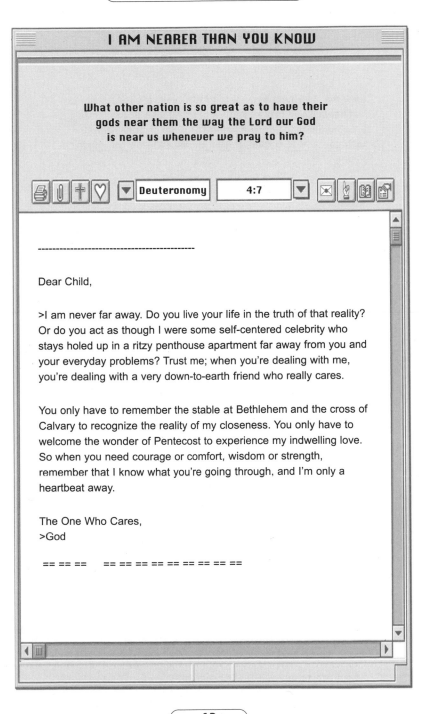

I AM NEARER THAN YOU KNOW

What other nation is so great as to have their gods near them the way the Lord our God is near us whenever we pray to him?

| Deuteronomy | 4:7 |

Dear Child,

>I am never far away. Do you live your life in the truth of that reality? Or do you act as though I were some self-centered celebrity who stays holed up in a ritzy penthouse apartment far away from you and your everyday problems? Trust me; when you're dealing with me, you're dealing with a very down-to-earth friend who really cares.

You only have to remember the stable at Bethlehem and the cross of Calvary to recognize the reality of my closeness. You only have to welcome the wonder of Pentecost to experience my indwelling love. So when you need courage or comfort, wisdom or strength, remember that I know what you're going through, and I'm only a heartbeat away.

The One Who Cares,
>God

== == ==   == == == == == == == == ==

CREATING BOUNDARIES

Children, obey your parents in the Lord, for this is right. "Honor your father and mother"—which is the first commandment with a promise—"that it may go well with you and that you may enjoy long life on the earth."

| Ephesians | 6:1–3 |

My Daughter,

>How important is teaching children to obey? Children gain a sense of security from knowing where their boundaries are, and teaching obedience is lovingly creating boundaries. When you lead your children to obey, you are leading them into a greater sense of security.

When you feel worn down and tired of the inevitable struggle that comes with disciplining, know that your efforts are worth it. I have given your children free will, and they may choose to resist your teaching. But if you've taught them lovingly and well, the confidence they will have in you and in themselves will far outweigh their temporary resistance. Stick with a loving plan of discipline. I am with you, my daughter.

Your Father and Theirs,
>God

== == ==   == == == == == == == == ==

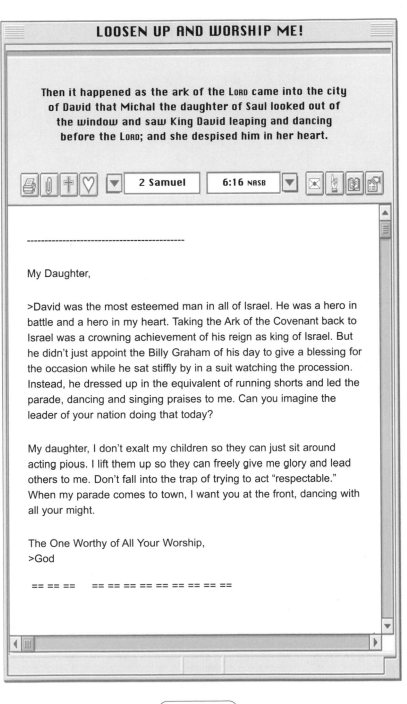

LOOSEN UP AND WORSHIP ME!

Then it happened as the ark of the LORD came into the city of David that Michal the daughter of Saul looked out of the window and saw King David leaping and dancing before the LORD; and she despised him in her heart.

2 Samuel | 6:16 NASB

My Daughter,

>David was the most esteemed man in all of Israel. He was a hero in battle and a hero in my heart. Taking the Ark of the Covenant back to Israel was a crowning achievement of his reign as king of Israel. But he didn't just appoint the Billy Graham of his day to give a blessing for the occasion while he sat stiffly by in a suit watching the procession. Instead, he dressed up in the equivalent of running shorts and led the parade, dancing and singing praises to me. Can you imagine the leader of your nation doing that today?

My daughter, I don't exalt my children so they can just sit around acting pious. I lift them up so they can freely give me glory and lead others to me. Don't fall into the trap of trying to act "respectable." When my parade comes to town, I want you at the front, dancing with all your might.

The One Worthy of All Your Worship,
>God

== == ==   == == == == == == == == ==

I HIRED YOU FOR THIS JOB

Serve wholeheartedly, as if you were serving the Lord, not men.

Ephesians	6:7

My Daughter,

>Some days when the work seems endless, when your boss is demanding and your loved ones act ungrateful, you may feel like running away from it all. Listen. You can look at your job on two levels. On one level you're serving human beings—boss, customers, family members. But on a higher plane, you're serving me. I am the one who placed you in this job, and I'll provide you with all you need to get it done.

So here's your mission, should you choose to accept it. Every morning get on your knees and say, "Okay, God, I'll live this day for you in your presence and for your glory. Fuel me. Equip me. Help me to do a great job for you."

Your Job Consultant,
>God

== == ==   == == == == == == == == ==

HOLD MY HAND

**All of you who held fast to the LORD
your God are still alive today.**

| Deuteronomy | 4:4 |

Dear Child,

>One of the first things you teach your young children is how to cross the street safely. "Look both ways for traffic and hold tight to my hand," you say. The "traffic" that threatens the safety of young people today includes some very deadly realities: violence, drugs, teen suicides, teen pregnancies, and religious cults.

How can your children "cross the street" of life safely? You need to warn them about the potential dangers. No need to get hysterical and overstate your case. Just calmly and sensibly show them the realities. Let them know you'll be there for them, and so will I. Teach them that rushing out into the "traffic" of life leads to death, but holding on to me and my truth leads to life.

The One You Hold on To,
>God

== == ==   == == == == == == == == ==

BE PREPARED

Put on the full armor of God so that you can take your stand against the devil's schemes. For our struggle is not against flesh and blood, but against the rulers, against the authorities, against the powers of this dark world and against the spiritual forces of evil in the heavenly realms.

Ephesians 6:11-12

Dear Child,

>What kind of general would send his soldiers into battle with no weapons, no strategy, and no information about enemy operations? He would either be cruel or stupid. Trust me, I am neither. As your Commander in Chief, I want you to be prepared. Life on planet Earth is quite literally a daily battle, but it's spiritual, not physical. It's a battle between good and evil, right and wrong, truth and lies. You will need my armor to stand against the enemy. So put on the helmet of salvation, the belt of truth, the breastplate of right living, and the shoes of good news. Take up the shield of faith and the sword of the Spirit. Get in the habit of praying effortlessly and trustingly. Now, follow me!

Your General,
>God

== == ==   == == == == == == == == ==

NOBODY'S PERFECT

We all stumble in many ways. If anyone is never
at fault in what he says, he is a perfect man,
able to keep his whole body in check.

James 3:2

Dear Child,

>Human beings are prone to blow it. Check the Bible. The only perfect person described in its pages is Jesus. Everyone else was a sinner. David had Uriah killed so he could sleep with his wife. Moses killed a man in a fight. Peter denied he knew the Lord. Paul watched in approval as Stephen was stoned to death. If human beings had been able to achieve sinlessness on their own, there would have been no need for the cross, and Jesus would have died for nothing.

So don't try to give your children, your husband, or your friends the impression that you're perfect. Learn to be vulnerable. Seek forgiveness for your own sins, and forgive others for theirs. That's Christianity 101.

Your Forgiving Father,
>God

== == ==   == == == == == == == == ==

GO FOR THE GOAL

Therefore, since we are surrounded by such a great cloud
of witnesses, let us throw off everything that hinders
and the sin that so easily entangles, and let us run
with perseverance the race marked out for us.

| Hebrews | 12:1 |

My Daughter,

>Have you ever watched Olympic runners in a race? They have
trained until there is not an extra ounce of fat on their bodies. They
are totally ready—totally focused on the goal of winning the race.

I want you to operate like those champions, my child, because you
are quite literally running the race of your life. I have set out a
challenging course for you to follow, but you are not alone. There's a
crowd of saints and angels in Heaven cheering you on, every step of
the way. "Go for it!" they shout. "Get up! You can do it," they yell when
you stumble. And who is yelling louder than anyone? I am!

Your Loving Coach,
>God

== == ==   == == == == == == == == ==

USE YOUR INFLUENCE

Observe [my decrees and laws] carefully, for this will show your wisdom and understanding to the nations, who will . . . say, "Surely this great nation is a wise and understanding people."

Deuteronomy | 4:6

My Child,

>You may not see yourself as a person of great influence; but trust me, you are! Whom do you influence? Obviously, your family first. You set the tone in your home. If you're calm, encouraging, humorous, and hopeful, these contagious attitudes will spread through your family like a healing balm.

You also influence other people, like your coworkers, your neighbors, the grocery checkout clerk, the waitress in the fast-food restaurant. As you live for me, your character will become apparent to others. My life will shine out of you in the most natural and loving way. And as it does, many of those in your field of influence will be drawn to me.

Your Indwelling Power,
>God

KEEP YOUR FOCUS

Let us hold unswervingly to the hope we profess, for he who promised is faithful.

| Hebrews | 10:23 |

My Dear Daughter,

>If the world were all you had to hope in, I'd feel sorry for you. The world I created is beautiful, I know, but it's also a world of disappointments. Things wear out and get lost. Investments fail to pay off. Political promises are breached. Even your most trusted friends and loved ones sometimes let you down.

But I am the loved one who will never let you down. My promises will never be breached. I am the investment that will always pay off and the hope that will never disappoint. So when life lets you down, turn to my love that will never fail and my kingdom that will never fall.

Your Faithful Father,
>God

== == ==   == == == == == == == == ==

YOU WERE MADE FOR THIS

From the very beginning God decided that those who came to him . . . should become like his Son, so that his Son would be the First, with many brothers.

Romans | **8:29** TLB

My Daughter,

>What is your job description as my child? It's to let me remake you into the image of my Son. Relax. I'm not asking you to be a perfect clone of Jesus. That's not possible. But if you'll let me fill you with my Spirit, you'll begin to bear a surprising family resemblance to Him. You'll find yourself spending your time more like he spent his and valuing the things he valued.

What did Jesus value? His top priorities were his relationships with me and with other people. So here's the game plan, my child. Open yourself to my Holy Spirit, and he'll begin to transform you more and more each day into a woman who's committed, just as Jesus was, to loving me and loving others.

The Love That Transforms,
>God

== == ==   == == == == == == == == ==

THE TREASURE OF MY PROMISES

You need to persevere so that when you have done the will of God, you will receive what he has promised.

| Hebrews | 10:36 |

My Daughter,

>My promises for you are like buried treasure, just waiting to be discovered. When you're sailing your ship in search of that treasure, don't be afraid of the rough winds of life or the troubled seas of circumstance. Keep moving toward the treasure of my promises, which never fail.

What promises am I talking about? The gold of my Word, the silver of my faithfulness, and the priceless gem of my presence, to mention just a few! Keep your sails up, my child, and stay on course.

The Promise Keeper,
>God

== == ==   == == == == == == == == ==

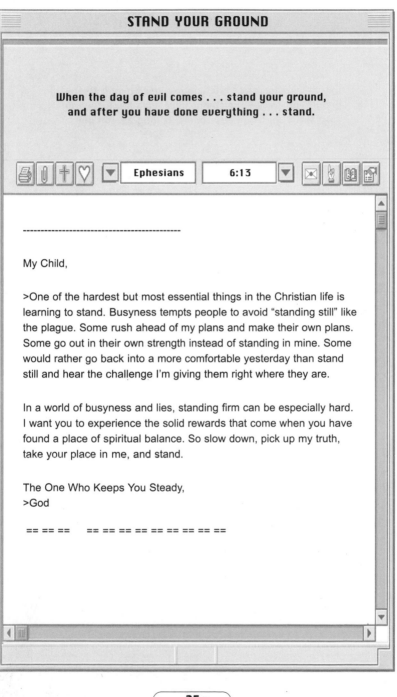

STAND YOUR GROUND

**When the day of evil comes . . . stand your ground,
and after you have done everything . . . stand.**

Ephesians 6:13

My Child,

>One of the hardest but most essential things in the Christian life is learning to stand. Busyness tempts people to avoid "standing still" like the plague. Some rush ahead of my plans and make their own plans. Some go out in their own strength instead of standing in mine. Some would rather go back into a more comfortable yesterday than stand still and hear the challenge I'm giving them right where they are.

In a world of busyness and lies, standing firm can be especially hard. I want you to experience the solid rewards that come when you have found a place of spiritual balance. So slow down, pick up my truth, take your place in me, and stand.

The One Who Keeps You Steady,
>God

== == ==   == == == == == == == == ==

KEEP ME ON YOUR MIND

> Only be careful, and watch yourselves closely so that
> you do not forget the things your eyes have seen or
> let them slip from your heart as long as you live.

Deuteronomy   **4:9**

My Child,

>I realize how frantic your life gets at times. In the midst of all the
rush and hurry, even the most important things can slip your mind.
But I encourage you never to forget how much I love you and how
much I've done for you. Don't let the mundane and the trivial rob
you of the amazing and the eternal. Recall my faithfulness.
Rehearse in your mind the good things I've done in your life.
Commit to spending time with me every day, and those quiet
moments will revitalize your outlook.

When you are mindful of my goodness, you will experience a
wellspring of joy bubbling up in you and overflowing to your family,
your friends, and all those around you.

The One Worth Remembering,
>God

== == ==   == == == == == == == == ==

TURN AROUND

This is what the Sovereign LORD, the Holy One of Israel,
says: "In repentance and rest is your salvation,
in quietness and trust is your strength."

| Isaiah | 30:15 |

Dear Child,

>Some people have the mistaken idea that to repent is to feel bad
about their sins. But to repent is not to *feel* something; it's to *do*
something. To repent is to turn around, to change your course and go
at life from a different direction.

Suppose you discovered that you had taken Jones Street when you
should have taken Smith Lane. Would it help you to feel bad about
your mistake? No. Until you turned around and changed directions,
you'd never reach your destination. So when you have sinned, come
to me and confess. I'll freely forgive you. Then take the important step
of repenting by turning your life around. I'll redirect you and steer you
toward your holy destination.

Your Loving Father,
>God

== == ==   == == == == == == == == ==

LEARN TO FORGIVE

Peter came to Jesus and asked, "Lord, how many times
shall I forgive my brother when he sins against me?
Up to seven times?" Jesus answered, "I tell you,
not seven times, but seventy-seven times."

Matthew | 18:21-22

My Child,

>Are you holding a grudge against someone you should be forgiving?
If so, then you and I need to talk. First of all, how many times has
Jesus forgiven your own failures and sins? Unnumbered times, right?
Now look at the person you're refusing to forgive. How much did
Jesus love that person? So much he was willing to go to the cross.
So who are you to be judge and jury?

Now think about this: how high was forgiveness on Jesus' agenda?
His words from the cross will give you the only answer you need.
"Father, forgive them." Oh, my daughter, you'll never be like Jesus
until you learn to forgive. Start today.

Your Forgiving Father,
>God

== == ==   == == == == == == == == ==

LET THE LIGHT SHINE IN

**As we obey this commandment, to love one another,
the darkness in our lives disappears and
the new light of life in Christ shines in.**

| 1 John | 2:8 TLB |

Dear Child,

>Love is the skylight of your spiritual home. It is the key that unlocks the windows of your heart to my light and warmth and healing. Love renews hope; it spreads peace; it illuminates the drab, lonely heart. Consider the beauty of this gift.

You are called not only to receive it, but you are also challenged to give it away. And as you do, my light pours into your life and the lives of those around you. As you love others, my richest blessings flow back to you and you are enabled to love more. Find every opportunity to love today, my child. Let the light shine in.

The Heart of Love,
>God

== == ==   == == == == == == == == ==

NEVER GIVE UP ON YOURSELF

There is now no condemnation awaiting those who belong to Christ Jesus.

| Romans | 8:1 TLB |

Dearest Child,

>There are two voices sounding off in your head when you blow it. Voice number one says, "Well, that's it. You've really done it now. Might as well throw in the towel." Recognize that line of reasoning? It's the enemy. His main goal is to get you to give up on yourself.

But there's another line of reasoning you'll hear in your head when you blow it. It's my still, small voice saying, "Get up, my child. I know you've fallen, but your mistakes are forgivable and your life is redeemable. Seek my forgiveness and trust my mercy. I don't condemn you and I won't give up on you. So never give up on yourself."

Tune out the lies of voice number one, my child, and listen to my voice of redemption!

Your Redeemer,
>God

== == ==   == == == == == == == == ==

ENDLESS STRENGTH

Be strong in the Lord and in his mighty power.

| Ephesians | 6:10 |

My Dear Child,

>Human strength eventually runs out. Sometimes even the greatest distance runners, after crossing the finish line, fall onto the grass gasping for breath. Champion discus throwers can hurl huge weights over incredible distances, but eventually they reach their limit.

My strength is different. There's no end to it. When you pray to me for help, I'm like lightning. I'm there before you say "amen." When the weight of your problems is holding you down, my arms lift it off you. And here's the kicker. I can empower *you* with *my* power, so why would you want to rely on your own? Don't go it alone, my child. Call on me.

The Empowering One,
>God

== == ==   == == == == == == == == ==

I'LL GIVE YOU SPIRIT EYES

Though our bodies are dying, our inner strength in the Lord is growing every day.

2 Corinthians	4:16 TLB

My Dear Daughter,

>Do you ever catch yourself looking at life through the world's distorted lenses? Do you see things all around you drying up, wearing out, withering and dying? Do you look in the mirror every birthday and observe the outer changes—a few more wrinkles, maybe a gray hair or two?

Oh, my child, if only you could catch a glimpse of yourself through my eyes of love. If only you could see the beautiful inner changes, the strength of character, the spiritual loveliness I see forming in you. These hidden qualities are precious in my sight. So throw away the world's flawed vision. I'll give you "Spirit eyes" to see yourself as you really are—more beautiful each day.

The Eyes of Love,
>God

== == ==   == == == == == == == == ==

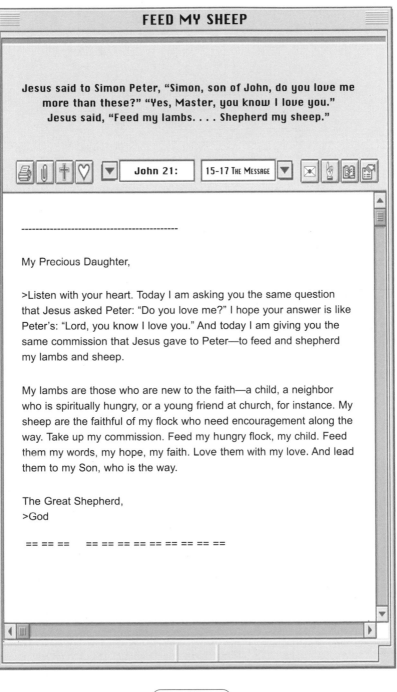

FEED MY SHEEP

Jesus said to Simon Peter, "Simon, son of John, do you love me more than these?" "Yes, Master, you know I love you." Jesus said, "Feed my lambs. . . . Shepherd my sheep."

John 21: | 15-17 The Message

My Precious Daughter,

>Listen with your heart. Today I am asking you the same question that Jesus asked Peter: "Do you love me?" I hope your answer is like Peter's: "Lord, you know I love you." And today I am giving you the same commission that Jesus gave to Peter—to feed and shepherd my lambs and sheep.

My lambs are those who are new to the faith—a child, a neighbor who is spiritually hungry, or a young friend at church, for instance. My sheep are the faithful of my flock who need encouragement along the way. Take up my commission. Feed my hungry flock, my child. Feed them my words, my hope, my faith. Love them with my love. And lead them to my Son, who is the way.

The Great Shepherd,
>God

== == ==   == == == == == == == == ==

STOP COMPARING

**With my own eyes I have seen
your salvation.**

| Luke | 2:30 NCV |

My Child,

>Do you ever look at well-known Christian women and think their faith is in a whole different league from yours? *They are the faithful greats,* you think. *I'm just a small-time Christian.* Listen. I don't grade my saints. I paid the same price to redeem you that I did to redeem the most prominent Christian speaker or theologian in the world. I paid the full kingdom entry fee—the sinless life of my Son.

So stop comparing yourself to others. Let me show you who you are in Christ. Let me show you your own salvation and how I want to use your gifts. Your faith in Jesus is what brought you into my family. You're precious in my sight!

Your Loving Father,
>God

== == ==   == == == == == == == == ==

A ONE-WORD ANSWER

**For it is by grace you have been saved, through faith—
and this not from yourselves, it is the gift of God—
not by works, so that no one can boast.**

| Ephesians | 2:8-9 |

Dear Child,

>I hope you know that you and I are going to be spending a long, long time together. Like—eternity! But suppose I were to ask how you know you're headed for Heaven. Would you answer, "Because I'm a good person—at least I know I'm better than a lot of people"? I'd be pretty disappointed in that answer.

You see, you can't earn a ticket to Heaven with good behavior. And being better than other people won't help at all, because I don't grade on the curve. I'm looking for a one-word answer to my heavenly question, and that word is "grace." Grace is love you didn't deserve and couldn't earn. Trusting Jesus and loving Him is what turns on the grace that makes Heaven your home.

Your Gracious Father,
>God

LEARN TO WALK

**The believers learned how to walk in the fear
of the Lord and in the comfort of the Holy Spirit.**

| Acts | 9:31 TLB |

My Daughter,

>Just like a baby learning to walk physically, you are learning to walk
spiritually. Don't be surprised if it doesn't come naturally at first. Don't
be discouraged if you fall now and then.

In the past the wisdom of the world guided your steps. Now my Son
will be your guide. He will lead you over uncharted roads into
unplanned adventures. In the past, maybe you relied on your own
little secret set of compulsive behaviors to give you balance and
comfort—like overeating or overworking or overspending. Now your
balance and comfort will come from my Spirit. Hold my hand as we
set out into each day together, and you'll discover the joy of walking
in the Spirit.

Your Father,
>God

== == ==   == == == == == == == == ==

MY HOME IS BEAUTIFUL

In my Father's house are many rooms; if it were
not so, I would have told you. I am going
there to prepare a place for you.

| John | 14:2 |

My Daughter,

>Use your imagination. Picture yourself approaching a gracious home on a sprawling green lawn. A shady front porch invites you to step through the door into a living room with huge windows that let in the afternoon sunlight. Gracing the tables are fresh flowers and framed photographs of loved ones. The tempting aroma of food fills the air, and you notice the dining table in the adjoining room is set with crystal, china, and silver. Someone speaks your name in a voice you recognize. You turn, and suddenly you're looking into eyes of grace and kindness. You're enfolded in a warm embrace. "Welcome, my daughter. You are home at last!"

This scene is not make-believe, my child. This is a picture of the love that waits for you in Heaven.

The One Who Will Greet You,
>God

== == ==   == == == == == == == == ==

THE SOIL OF FAITH

I wait for the LORD, my soul waits,
and in his word I put my hope.

| Psalm | 130:5 |

My Daughter,

>Many people equate waiting with wasting time. They see times of inactivity as a total write-off. But I see waiting as the soil of faith in which your spirit can grow sure and strong.

What will you learn when you're willing to wait? You'll learn that you don't have all the answers, and in time you'll find that I do. You'll learn that action, if it's the wrong action, can be worse than no action at all. You'll learn that faith is a dance, a dance in which I must lead. You'll learn to trust my character while you're waiting for my guidance, and you'll learn to lean into my love even when it's silent. So center your spirit on me and hope in my Word as you wait.

The One Worth Waiting For,
>God

== == ==   == == == == == == == == ==

STAY CONNECTED

I am the vine; you are the branches. If a man
remains in me and I in him, he will bear much fruit;
apart from me you can do nothing.

John 15:5

Dear Child of Mine,

>You've heard it before, but do you get it? I'm the vine; you're the
branch through which the "sap" of my life is meant to flow and grow
into good and life-giving things.

But there's an important difference between you and a branch. A
branch has no choice. It has to stay connected to the vine. You have
a free will. Anytime you choose, you can unplug yourself and start
operating out of your human nature. But when you rip the branch of
your life out of the vine of my love, all the exciting things I was
planning to do through you will dry up. Only when you stay connected
to my Spirit and me will your life continue to grow into what I want it to
be. So stay connected, my daughter.

The Vine,
>God

== == ==   == == == == == == == == ==

WORSHIP, THEN WORK

Come, let us bow down in worship, let us kneel before the LORD our Maker; for he is our God and we are the people of his pasture, the flock under his care.

Psalm | 95:6-7

Dear Daughter,

>When the children of Israel returned to Jerusalem after years in exile, their first order of business was to build an altar. They had learned there was nothing more important than worshiping me.

Have you learned that all-important truth? Have you made that commitment? Look, I know you're busy. I know it's hard to fit in a time for me. But I assure you that whatever you have to do today will go better after you've taken time to worship. Put me first, and I will help you prioritize those other commitments. You'll be amazed at the sense of peace that will flood your heart as you give me first place. So here's the formula: first worship, then work.

The One You Worship,
>God

== == ==   == == == == == == == == ==

GET ON WITH THE JOY!

**We have different gifts, according to
the grace given us.**

| Romans | | 12:6 | |

My Child,

>Why are you so willing to see your shortcomings and so reluctant to
see your gifts? Suppose you cook a delicious, gourmet meal for a
friend. Eagerly you seat her at the table, waiting for her reaction. She
takes her first bite. She chews. She wrinkles up her nose and whines,
"It's underdone in the middle, and it needs more seasoning!" Wouldn't
you feel hurt and put down?

Well, that's the way I feel when you constantly criticize yourself and
refuse to live in the amazing destiny I've mapped out for you. I made
you. I'm proud of you. You're here for a reason. It's time to
acknowledge your awesome gifts and get on with the joy of using
them for me.

The Gift-giver,
>God

== == ==   == == == == == == == == ==

NO WONDER THEY CALL IT AMAZING!

He said to me, "My grace is sufficient for you,
for my power is made perfect in weakness." Therefore
I will boast all the more gladly about my weaknesses,
so that Christ's power may rest on me.

| 2 Corinthians | 12:9 |

My Daughter,

>You've probably heard that my grace is amazing. It definitely is. It's like a spring of water that never runs dry. There's always enough for whatever problems arise. Health problems? My grace is sufficient. Finances? My grace is sufficient. Relationship problems? My grace is sufficient.

In fact, every circumstance that shows your weakness only serves to reveal my strength. Every situation that shows your inadequacy only serves to reveal my adequacy. So don't let troubles drive you to despair. Let them drive you to prayer. There's abundant grace for whatever you need. No wonder they call it amazing!

The Grace-giver,
>God

== == ==   == == == == == == == == ==

WHEN YOU LEAST DESERVED IT

**God demonstrates his own love for us in this:
While we were still sinners, Christ died for us.**

Romans   5:8

O My Daughter,

>Could you ever have done anything good enough to merit what Jesus did for you on Calvary? When you were at your most unlovable, he went to the cross with love in his heart and you on his mind. He didn't think to himself, *Well, maybe one of these days when she finally measures up, I'll die for her. Maybe when she finally gets her closets organized and gets her kids to behave, I'll get nailed to a cross for her.* How absurd!

Jesus chose Calvary when you least deserved it—in the darkness of your sin and the frailty of your faith. So open your hands and your heart and freely accept what he has freely given—his grace and love for you.

The Father of the Crucified,
>God

== == ==   == == == == == == == == ==

ONE IN THE SPIRIT

**He who unites himself with the Lord is one
with him in spirit.**

▼ 1 Corinthians   6:17   ▼

My Child,

>Is this one of those days when you feel fragmented, like a huge
jigsaw puzzle with all the pieces scattered on the floor? You may feel
that way, but the truth is, you're not fragmented. When you trusted
your life to me, we became one in spirit.

In your body, in your unique personality, you still function as a separate
person. But in your spirit, the deepest part of who you are, you and I
are united. Just as Jesus said, "My Father and I are one," so are we.
My Spirit in your spirit is the answer to that fractured feeling. So learn
to walk in the Spirit, and watch the puzzle come together.

The Indwelling One,
>God

    == == ==   == == == == == == == == ==

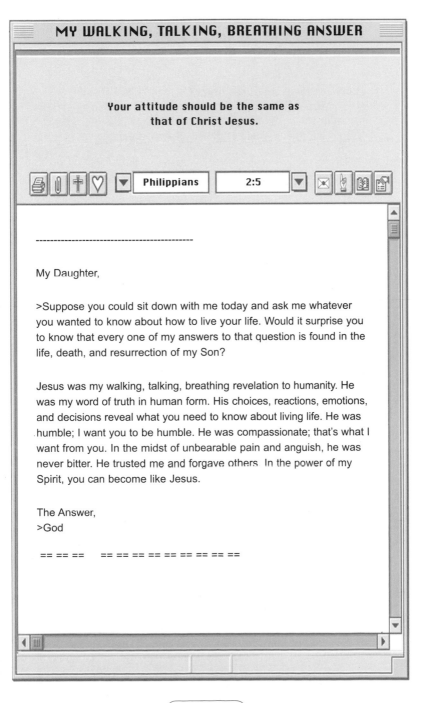

MY WALKING, TALKING, BREATHING ANSWER

**Your attitude should be the same as
that of Christ Jesus.**

Philippians   2:5

My Daughter,

>Suppose you could sit down with me today and ask me whatever
you wanted to know about how to live your life. Would it surprise you
to know that every one of my answers to that question is found in the
life, death, and resurrection of my Son?

Jesus was my walking, talking, breathing revelation to humanity. He
was my word of truth in human form. His choices, reactions, emotions,
and decisions reveal what you need to know about living life. He was
humble; I want you to be humble. He was compassionate; that's what I
want from you. In the midst of unbearable pain and anguish, he was
never bitter. He trusted me and forgave others. In the power of my
Spirit, you can become like Jesus.

The Answer,
>God

== == ==   == == == == == == == == ==

POWER AT YOUR FINGERTIPS

We have the word of the prophets made more certain, and you will do well to pay attention to it, as to a light shining in a dark place, until the day dawns and the morning star rises in your hearts.

2 Peter 1:19

My Daughter,

>Today, in the midst of whatever you're going through, let my Word shine in. What are you dealing with today? (Big bills—no money? Major relationship on the blink? Yearly checkup—bad diagnosis?) My Word is waiting to speak. Or maybe you're just dealing with the nagging frustrations and interruptions of normal life (lost keys, flat tire, irritating coworker, colicky baby). My Word applies.

But here's the hitch: just as you have to turn on the light switch to get the lamp to do its job, you'll have to pick up my Word, open its pages, read, and believe, if you want it to help you. So don't wait. You've got power at your fingertips.

The Light,
>God

== == ==   == == == == == == == == ==

QUESTIONS LEAD TO ANSWERS

Then he said to Thomas, "Put your finger
into my hands. Put your hand into my side.
Don't be faithless any longer. Believe!"

John   **20:27** TLB

My Daughter,

>There is nothing shameful about questions. If you never had a single
question or doubt as a Christian, you would be very unusual. Questions
lead to answers. Doubts lead to belief.

When the other disciples told Thomas they had seen Jesus, he
doubted. "Unless I see him for myself, I won't believe," he said. Jesus
heard the sincerity of his friend's questioning, and he supplied the
experience that put those questions to rest.

Are you struggling with some doubt today? Is there an experience
that others have had that you have not had? Talk honestly to Jesus
and to me. Let us answer your questions. Let us touch you and put
your doubts to rest.

The Love That Leads to Faith,
>God

== == ==   == == == == == == == == ==

I'M READING YOUR HEART

He has showed you, O man, what is good. And what does the Lord require of you? To act justly and to love mercy and to walk humbly with your God.

| Micah | | 6:8 | |

My Child,

>I created you to make a difference in the world. Does that mean I expect you to be elected president or head up a huge corporation or spearhead a missionary effort? Those things are certainly possible, but you don't have to achieve big things to please me.

I want you to live your life honestly, without a lot of fanfare. Respect other people, and treat them fairly. Show mercy and simple kindness as Jesus did. And walk with me a day at a time. The movers and shakers of your society may rack up political and financial power, but I'm not impressed. I'm reading your heart, not your bankbook. It's deeds of quiet humility that earn interest in my kingdom.

The One Whose Will Is Perfect,
>God

== == ==   == == == == == == == == ==

SPEAK FREELY

You will receive power when the Holy Spirit comes on you;
and you will be my witnesses in Jerusalem, and in all
Judea and Samaria, and to the ends of the earth.

Acts 1:8

Dear Child,

>Do you feel shy and little bit tongue-tied when you speak about your faith? That's not surprising. When faith is genuine, talking about it taps into some pretty powerful emotions. Never be ashamed of your emotions.

Just pray before you speak and let my Holy Spirit take over. He'll give you his power and his clarity. He'll help you speak with such simple, honest candor that those who hear your words will be moved by what you say. They'll see something in your life that they'll want in their own. So, don't worry about having the perfect words. Trust my Spirit and speak freely.

The Communicator,
>God

== == ==   == == == == == == == == ==

A WHOLEHEARTED ATTITUDE

**My servant Caleb has a different spirit
and follows me wholeheartedly.**

| Numbers | 14:24 |

My Daughter,

>What kind of attitude are you looking for in your relationship with
your children? Is it a whiney, half-baked response—a shrug and a
sassy reply? Are you pleased when they drag their feet, hesitating to
do what you say? No, I feel pretty sure that the child who pleases
you is the one who follows your directions wholeheartedly, speedily,
and cheerfully.

It's exactly the same with me. Your vibrant faith and your
wholehearted obedience are good ways to show me your love. Those
attitudes let me know you're willing to go with my program and trust
me for the outcome even when you don't understand it all. Follow me
wholeheartedly, my child.

Your Father,
>God

== == ==   == == == == == == == == ==

THE MAKEOVER BUSINESS

We . . . are being transformed into his likeness with ever-increasing glory, which comes from the Lord, who is the Spirit.

2 Corinthians	3:18

My Daughter,

>Do you ever read those magazine articles about beauty makeovers in which flattering clothes and makeup transform a woman who thought of herself as homely into a surprisingly attractive version of her former self?

Well, I'm in the makeover business, too—only my makeovers are internal rather than external. I transform character, strengthen integrity, and purify motives. The more you trust me, the more room my Holy Spirit will have to do his work in you. The closer you follow me, the more you will resemble my Son. So put your life in my hands, and you'll love the changes you begin to see in yourself!

The Master of the Makeover
>God

== == ==   == == == == == == == == ==

YOU ARE ENTERING A WAR ZONE

We demolish arguments and every pretension that sets itself up against the knowledge of God, and we take captive every thought to make it obedient to Christ.

2 Corinthians   **10:5**

My Daughter,

>Suppose you heard sirens screaming and a sound system blaring the news that you were being attacked. You'd probably do something to get ready. Well, today you *will* be involved in a battle, but the battleground will be your mind. You're already equipped with truth. You know you're my child, and nothing can separate you from my love.

But today you may hear little lies in your mind waging war against that truth. They might try to tell you I'm not real or I don't love you or I can't forgive you. That's just the enemy talking. When you hear him, tune him out and call on me. I'll boost your faith so that you can demolish his lies and put every thought in the hands of my Son.

The Overcoming Truth,
>God

== == ==   == == == == == == == == ==

A SEEKER AND A SAVER

**The Son of Man came to seek and
to save what was lost.**

| Luke | 19:10 |

Dear Child,

>Most people have heard that Jesus came to save people from the evil in the world and the wrong in their own hearts. But some who haven't read the Bible aren't familiar with the small print in that good news.

Jesus didn't just show up on planet Earth and set up shop, waiting around for people to come and ask for his services. Jesus went out looking for the ones who needed him. He went looking behind every lame excuse, every selfish motive, every arrogant ambition. And he's still looking for everyone who needs to be saved. He stands at the edge of their heartbreak or their affluence or their loneliness, calling to them: "Come to me."

Your Father and His,
>God

== == ==   == == == == == == == == ==

THE BEST KIND OF FUNERAL

When the perishable has been clothed with the imperishable, and the mortal with immortality, then the saying that is written will come true: "Death has been swallowed up in victory."

| 1 Corinthians | 15:54 |

Dear Daughter,

>You probably wouldn't choose a funeral as your favorite form of entertainment. No one looks forward to saying goodbye to a loved one. But there is a huge difference between the death of one who has loved me and the death of one who has loved the world. The death of the worldly man or woman has a sad finality to it. But the death of the one who has loved and lived for me is victorious. Even in the midst of sadness, there can be great joy, because grief is infused with the reality that this child of mine has passed through the doorway between mortality and immortality.

So when death separates you from one of my saints, remember, you'll be seeing him or her again.

The Victorious One,
>God

== == ==   == == == == == == == == ==

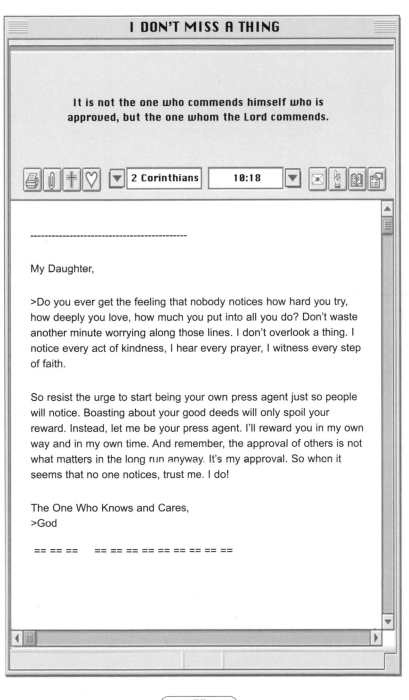

I DON'T MISS A THING

It is not the one who commends himself who is approved, but the one whom the Lord commends.

| 2 Corinthians | 10:18 |

My Daughter,

>Do you ever get the feeling that nobody notices how hard you try, how deeply you love, how much you put into all you do? Don't waste another minute worrying along those lines. I don't overlook a thing. I notice every act of kindness, I hear every prayer, I witness every step of faith.

So resist the urge to start being your own press agent just so people will notice. Boasting about your good deeds will only spoil your reward. Instead, let me be your press agent. I'll reward you in my own way and in my own time. And remember, the approval of others is not what matters in the long run anyway. It's my approval. So when it seems that no one notices, trust me. I do!

The One Who Knows and Cares,
>God

== == ==   == == == == == == == == ==

I HOLD THE TITLE

**You were bought at a price.
Therefore honor God with your body.**

1 Corinthians	6:20

Dear Child of Mine,

>Driving your car can become second nature. Most of the time you don't even think about it. But suppose a wealthy friend loaned you her shiny new Mercedes. Wouldn't you suddenly find yourself taking much better care of this swanky set of wheels?

Here's what I'm getting at. You are like the Mercedes. You are very valuable, and you are not your own. I bought and paid for you with the blood of my Son. And your body is only on loan to you for your lifetime. So remember who owns your body as you take care of it—as you choose what to eat and drink, how much rest you need, and what thoughts to entertain. And by the way, be sure to let my Holy Spirit do the driving.

The One Who Holds the Title,
>God

== == ==   == == == == == == == == ==

ANGER CAN BE TOXIC

**In your anger do not sin; when you are on
your beds, search your hearts and be silent.**

Psalm | 4:4

My Daughter,

>Have you ever seen a chemical plant pumping noxious gases into
the atmosphere? The unfortunate result is that the atmosphere is
polluted and people breathe poison.

Anger is like that. It can pollute the atmosphere of your home when
you let it explode. There's nothing wrong with feeling angry, but a
venomous outburst can do damage.

What do I suggest? Wait. Silently think and pray about what you're
feeling and why. Many times what really lies beneath your anger is a
secret stash of hurt feelings. Once you understand your anger, ask
me to help you approach the one who has hurt or angered you. I'll
give you words of reason and reconciliation.

The Ultimate Peacemaker,
>God

== == ==   == == == == == == == == ==

JUMPING THROUGH HOOPS

Christ's love compels us.

2 Corinthians 5:14

Dear Daughter,

>What compels you to get out of bed in the morning? What motivates you to do your work? Are you still trying to live up to your parents' overachievement expectations? Are you trying to be the Martha Stewart of your neighborhood? Are you trying to be the super-mom who can do it all—raise perfect children, have the ideal marriage, and outperform everyone at work? No wonder you fall into bed at night exhausted.

Go back to square one, my child, and examine your motives. Why are you jumping through all of these hoops? Invite Jesus to be the motive behind all you do, and you'll feel your weariness lifting. Listen to his words: "Come to me . . . and I'll give you rest."

The Love That Compels You,
>God

== == ==   == == == == == == == == ==

BE AN EXCELLENT GIVER

Just as you excel in everything . . . see that you also excel in this grace of giving.

2 Corinthians — 8:7

Dear Child of Mine,

>I want you to excel in everything—even giving. What is an excellent giver? An excellent giver lives with open hands and a willing heart. An excellent giver is tuned in to my Spirit as well as to the needs of others. When she feels my Spirit nudging her to give, she follows instructions. An excellent giver knows that all of her belongings really belong to me, and that giving is merely allowing me to shift my resources from one of my children to another. An excellent giver gives time, attention, affection, and affirmation as well as money. And when she is on the receiving end, she receives with a thankful heart.

The Ultimate Giver of the Perfect Gift,
>God

== == ==   == == == == == == == == ==

A FAMILY OF FAITH

We have heard with our ears, O God; our fathers have told us what you did in their days, in days long ago.

| Psalm | 44:1 |

My Child,

>How did you first hear about me? From a book? A sermon? The words of a friend? Or was faith handed down through the generations in your family?

I love to work in families—to be the tie that binds parents, children, husbands, wives, and siblings together through good times and bad. I love to build an eternal road over which whole families can travel one at a time into the open arms of my kingdom.

If you're the first one in your family to be a believer, begin praying for your family members now. In my time, I will show you how and when to share your faith with them. Trust me and believe. I will use your prayer to make yours a family of faith.

The Father of Your Faith,
>God

== == ==   == == == == == == == == ==

THE REAL WINNERS

**Blessed are the poor in spirit,
for theirs is the kingdom of heaven.**

Matthew | 5:3

My Daughter,

>How many people come to me in times of health, prosperity, and blessing? A few do. But many more seem to find me in times of failure and despair. When you're down, that's when you realize it's time to look up. When you're at the end of your rope, that's when you find yourself at the foot of the cross.

Jesus once said, "Blessed are the poor in spirit, for theirs is the kingdom of heaven." He knew that the poor in spirit, the bottomed-out, end-of-the-rope crowd, have a spiritual advantage over the top-of-the-world crowd. The top-of-the-world crowd believe they're in control. But the poor in spirit know they need me. That's why they're the real winners.

The Kingdom-giver,
>God

== == ==   == == == == == == == == ==

AN EQUAL OPPORTUNITY SAVIOR

He came and preached peace to you who were far away and peace to those who were near. For through him we both have access to the Father by one Spirit.

Ephesians | 2:17–18

Dear Child,

>Jesus is an equal opportunity Savior. When he came to earth bringing my message of peace, it wasn't just for the super-religious. (In fact, the super-religious frustrated him the most. He saw right through their pious posing to their hidden pride.) Jesus came for everyone. He brought the good news that anyone can have a relationship with me.

Are you near me today? Do you know you're my child? Or are you far away? Do you feel uncomfortable or unworthy in my presence. The truth is, if it weren't for Jesus, no one could approach me with confidence. But because of him everyone can. So come to me today from wherever you are—however near or far.

The One Who Waits,
>God

== == ==   == == == == == == == == ==

THE RESCUE NET

On my arm they will trust.

| Isaiah | 51:5 NKJV |

My Precious Daughter,

>Does it seem at times that you're walking a tightrope of anxiety over a sea of bad news? Daily headlines reporting world hunger, racial unrest, drugs, violence, international conflict, and a fluctuating economy leave you a little shaky.

I want you to learn to walk confidently. I want you to know that my arms are the rescue net beneath all of life's uncertainty. Whatever situation the world is in, you can trust in my protection and abide in my peace. When you're walking with me, trusting in me, and obeying me, you can't fall further than I am able to catch you. So when headlines deliver bad news, focus on this bit of good news. I am with you. And I'm in it for the long haul.

Your Rescue Net,
>God

== == ==   == == == == == == == == ==

I'M A DAD

To the LORD I cry aloud, and he answers me
from his holy hill. I lie down and sleep;
I wake again, because the LORD sustains me.

Psalm   3:4-5

Dear Daughter,

>You may have a mental image of me as CEO of the universe—
frantically dispatching troops of angels, keeping the stars on course,
holding back floods. I want you to change your image of me from a
stressed corporate executive in a three-piece suit to a dad who is
hanging out with you at home in blue jeans and a T-shirt.

I'm here to share your sorrows and your joys—to celebrate your
successes and grieve your losses. I'm never too busy to hear and to
help with your problems. I love your children even more than you do. I
want your marriage to succeed even more than you do. Bring
everything, good or bad, to the Dad who loves you. Freely pour out
your heart. I am never too busy to hear you and be with you.

Your Dad,
>God

== == ==   == == == == == == == == ==

HOPE CHANGES EVERYTHING

Brothers, we do not want you to . . .
grieve like the rest of men, who have no hope.

| 1 Thessalonians | 4:13 |

Dear Child of Mine,

>If life came in a package, one to a customer, the contents of each package would vary, but each would contain some pain and some grief. No one is exempt from those realities. But when you put your trust in me, I gave you a gift that can alter every negative ingredient in life's package. It is the gift of hope.

Hope is the rising song of victory breaking through the silence of defeat. Hope touches the winter of the heart with the springtime of new beginnings. Hope lifts the promise of eternity in the face of death. So when you're walking through a tough time, reach into the package of your life and seize my gift of hope. It will see you through to the other side.

Your Hope,
>God

== == ==   == == == == == == == == ==

CELEBRATE!

Let them give thanks to the Lord for his unfailing love and his wonderful deeds for men.

| Psalm | 107:21 |

Dear Child,

>When David brought the ark of my presence back and set it in the middle of my people, they rejoiced. They sang and danced and gave thanks. They remembered all the times I had blessed them and rescued them.

How long has it been since you have experienced a real surge of joy? How long since you have celebrated my goodness in your life? If you're not celebrating my love today, it may be because you need to recommit your life to me. You may need to return me to my rightful place in the center of your heart. Just as the return of the ark to its rightful place resulted in worship and celebration, the return of my peace and hope in your life will do the same thing.

The Lord of the Celebration,
>God

== == ==   == == == == == == == == ==

A NEW PORTRAIT

You do not stay angry forever but delight to show mercy.

| Micah | 7:18 |

My Daughter,

>When you picture my face, is it scowling and angry? Is it cruel and vindictive? If that's the way you see me, you need to let me paint a new portrait of myself in your heart.

Let me show you my eyes of compassion—eyes that see beyond your failings and your faults to your strengths, your gifts, and your tender heart. Let me show you my scarred hands of healing, my heart that hears your every prayer, my voice that speaks comfort, encouragement, forgiveness, and hope. Let me show you my arms that ache to welcome you into my presence. If your picture of me is wrong, how can your relationship with me be right? Let me show you who I really am, my child.

Your Merciful Father,
>God

== == ==   == == == == == == == == ==

KEEP YOUR GUARD UP!

**If you think you are standing firm,
be careful that you don't fall!**

| 1 Corinthians | 10:12 |

Dear Child,

>When is a mountain climber at the greatest point of risk? Paradoxically, it may not be on a highly dangerous peak, since that is where he is using extra caution. Instead, he may be more prone to lose his footing in a less dangerous place where he throws caution to the wind and gets careless.

The same is true in the spiritual life. You probably exercise extra caution at times of high temptation. You call on me, and I help you stand. But when things are cruising along pretty well, it's easy to let your guard down and slide right off some spiritual slope. Don't let this happen, my child. Don't let your guard down. You need me every day in every situation.

The One Who Helps You Stand,
>God

== == ==   == == == == == == == == ==

DON'T LEAVE HOME WITHOUT ME

**In all your ways acknowledge him,
and he will make your paths straight.**

| Proverbs | 3:6 |

My Daughter,

>When pioneers set out to explore a new land, there were no maps to rely on. That's why they never left home without an indispensable little instrument known as a compass. They would set their general direction, and many times during the journey they would check the compass to make sure they were on course.

You are on a journey, too. No one else on earth has ever traveled exactly the same path I have charted for you. The surest way to stay on course is to constantly acknowledge me in all you do. Speak to me; listen for me; check your bearings against my Word, and your foot will stay on course. This is an adventure! Aren't you glad we're in it together?

Your Compass,
>God

== == ==   == == == == == == == == ==

GO WITH MY PROGRAM

Do not be wise in your own eyes;
fear the Lord and shun evil.

Proverbs   **3:7**

My Child,

>Are you following your own personal life plan? Have you said things
like, "I'll marry at this point; I'll have children here; I'll concentrate on
my career at this point" and so on? Your plan of action may seem
very wise according to your view of things. But it's like the old saying:
"You can't see the forest for the trees." You are too close to your own
life to have the perspective you need.

I am over you, beside you, and within you, which gives me a unique
perspective. What's more, I'm the one who created you, and I know
what's best for you. So don't go with your own program. Trust me to
show you mine. Then follow it.

The One Who Knows What's Best,
>God

== == ==   == == == == == == == == ==

DON'T WEAR YOURSELF OUT

They weary themselves with sinning.

🖨 📎 ✝ ♡ ▼ | Jeremiah | 9:5 | ▼ | ✉ ✋ 📖 🖼

My Precious Child,

>Have you ever found yourself riding a wave of gossip—making harmful comments about another person without ever intending to? After the moment passes, a spiritual weariness comes over you. Do you know why? There is nothing more exhausting than sin. You were not made to harm others with words or deeds. You were not made to assault the character of another person.

To sin is to swim against the current of my will, and that is certain to wear you out every time. My way is rest and peace, and you can find it only by trusting my Son. Don't wear yourself out, my child. Sin is never worth the price you pay.

The Way of Rest,
>God

== == ==   == == == == == == == == ==

I'LL STILL BE YOUR DADDY

Even to your old age and gray hairs I am he, I am he who will sustain you. I have made you and I will carry you; I will sustain you and I will rescue you.

| Isaiah | 46:4 |

Dear Child,

>Are your friends planning a "black balloon" party for your birthday this year? Are they making jokes about having to call the fire department when they light all the candles on your cake? Listen. Don't buy into the world's view of getting a year older.

Don't you know that you will always be my little girl—the apple of my eye and the delight of my heart? Your beauty is ageless and your value is timeless. So see yourself through eyes of love, as I see you. Decorate your heart with balloons of many colors, and rejoice in another year of living as my child.

Your Heavenly Dad,
>God

== == ==   == == == == == == == == ==

PRACTICE HEAVEN

**Set your minds on things above,
not on earthly things [below].**

| | | | | | Colossians | 3:2 | | | | | |

My Child,

>Since you will be spending eternity in Heaven, why don't you begin
practicing Heaven here and now? Live with your mind in the stars and
out of the gutter. Live in perpetual hope rather than perpetual worry.

I am here for you now, placing heavenly things in your life. I am
surrounding you with eternal treasures. I am drying your tears and
healing your hurts. I am strengthening you in your weakness and
filling you in your emptiness. Since I am doing these heavenly things
for you, I want you to start practicing peace and praise and
completeness in every earthly circumstance, for that is the climate in
which you'll spend eternity.

Your Heaven on Earth,
>God

== == ==   == == == == == == == == ==

A DIFFERENT KIND OF FATHER

I will remember the covenant I made with you in the days of your youth, and I will establish an everlasting covenant with you.

| Ezekiel | 16:60 |

My Daughter,

>What kind of father did you have growing up? Was he forgetful and frequently preoccupied with work? Did he ever miss your birthday or forget promises he had made? If you had a father like that, don't get him mixed up with me.

I'm not a forgetful Father. I remember the day I created you, and I remember when you chose to take your first spiritual steps. I have been right with you at every important event in your life, cheering you on. I am never too busy working to sit and talk with my precious daughter. And the things I have promised you, I will surely fulfill. Trust me, my daughter, to be a good and faithful father—the Father you have always needed.

Your Covenant Keeper,
>God

== == ==   == == == == == == == == ==

GO UNDER MY BANNER

His banner over me is love.

Song of Songs   2:4

My Daughter,

>When medieval knights went off to battle, they went under the banner of the king they served. I am your Father and your King. As you go out into the everyday circumstances of your day, go under the banner of my love. Under the banner of love, you will be equipped to care for the needy, to stand for the disenfranchised, and to overcome the opposition of the enemy. There are people out there dying just to know me. There's a world out there just waiting to be saved. Go under the banner of my love, my child. Go out in the name of my Son, Jesus, who is love.

Your Father and King,
>God

== == ==   == == == == == == == == ==

ENJOY THE PROCESS

Christ loved the church and gave himself up for her . . . to present her to himself as a radiant church, without stain or wrinkle or any other blemish, but holy and blameless.

Ephesians 5:25-27

My Dear Child,

>You will be in the workshop of my love today. I am shaping you into my own creation. I will be using all the troubling, irritating things that happen to you to sand off your rough edges and make you more like Jesus.

Don't worry if you seem to be a long way from finished. Just keep your eyes on me and believe that I have the vision and ability to complete you perfectly. And be patient. All change that is worthwhile is gradual. If you stay in my masterful hands, every day you'll see more of my work in you. And every day you'll know Jesus better as you become more like him.

The One Who Perfects You,
>God

== == ==   == == == == == == == == ==

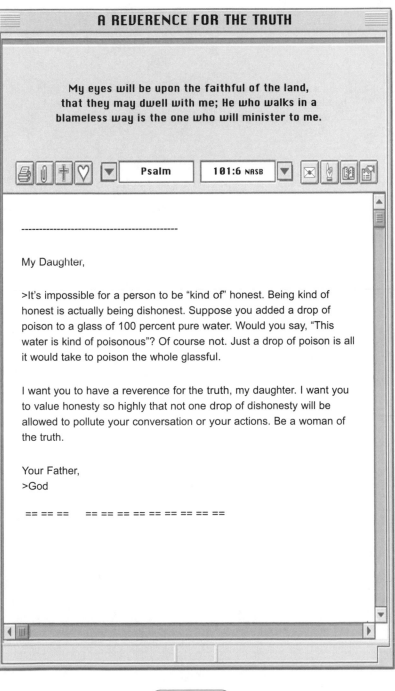

A REVERENCE FOR THE TRUTH

My eyes will be upon the faithful of the land,
that they may dwell with me; He who walks in a
blameless way is the one who will minister to me.

Psalm | **101:6 NASB**

My Daughter,

>It's impossible for a person to be "kind of" honest. Being kind of honest is actually being dishonest. Suppose you added a drop of poison to a glass of 100 percent pure water. Would you say, "This water is kind of poisonous"? Of course not. Just a drop of poison is all it would take to poison the whole glassful.

I want you to have a reverence for the truth, my daughter. I want you to value honesty so highly that not one drop of dishonesty will be allowed to pollute your conversation or your actions. Be a woman of the truth.

Your Father,
>God

== == ==   == == == == == == == == ==

THE FULLNESS OF CHRIST LIVES IN YOU

In Christ all the fullness of the Deity lives in
bodily form, and you have been given fullness in Christ,
who is the head over every power and authority.

| Colossians | 2:9-10 |

My Dear Child,

>All you need and ever have needed and ever will need is in my Son. Your complete identity, your confidence, your hope, your peace in the midst of conflict, as well as your purpose for living are in him, and he is in you. All you seek, you find in him. His Spirit indwells you with his gifts, his grace, his heart of love.

Every day of your life should be a powerful affirmation of this mystery. Every choice and action should ring with this good news. Your work should proclaim it wordlessly and your words should shout it from the rooftops: "The fullness of Christ is in me!"

The Father of Jesus,
>God

== == ==   == == == == == == == == ==

EMBRACE MY PLAN

We also rejoice in our sufferings, because
we know that suffering produces perseverance;
perseverance, character; and character, hope.

| Romans | 5:3-4 |

My Child,

>Have you ever seen weight lifters work out? They lift heavy weights
in order to have big muscles. If they lifted only small weights, they'd
have puny muscles.

I'm in the process of building you up in the Spirit. If there were no
hard times, no suffering in your life, you'd be a spiritual weakling.
That's why I'm asking you to rejoice in every struggle; I know it will
ultimately result in your strength. So, don't hide from my plans for
you. Accept every struggle as if it were a physical workout, and
celebrate the spiritual changes you see. Trust me, my child. I've been
building spiritual giants for a long time.

Your Personal Trainer,
>God

== == ==   == == == == == == == == ==

IN THE LAND OF SUFFERING

**God has made me fruitful in
the land of my suffering.**

| Genesis | 41:52 |

Dear Daughter,

>In the land of your suffering, in the soil of your trouble, a fruit of
unexpected sweetness will grow. In that land, when you need me most,
you will find me; when you pray, I will hear you. And even when my
answers seem far away, you will wait on me. Though others may not
understand, you will trust me. You will grow in grace and knowledge.

And when your heart is healed, you will return from that land of
suffering by a new route, bringing your gift of healing to others.
Through you, the fruit of healing that grew in the midst your pain will
multiply and spring up to bring healing to others who are suffering.

Your Healer and Comforter,
>God

== == ==   == == == == == == == == ==

THE DEATH THAT LEADS TO FREEDOM

**In the same way, count yourselves dead
to sin but alive to God in Christ Jesus.**

Romans **6:11**

My Child,

>In Jesus, to live is to die. What do I mean by that? In order to enjoy your new life in Christ, you're going to have to die to your old selfish life. Though it's painful, death to the selfish life brings incredible freedom—freedom from pride, jealousy, lust, lying, fear, and so much more!

Everyone knows a dead woman can't be prideful or jealous. A dead woman can't lust after money or possessions. A dead woman isn't tempted to stretch the truth to impress others. She can't be anxious or selfish or mean-spirited, because she's dead as a coffin nail. So why not get on with the funeral? Say good-bye to the old self-life and let me show you the freedom and joy of true life in my Son.

The Lord of Life,
>God

== == ==   == == == == == == == == ==

PUT YOUR EAR TO MY HEART

**"They shall be mine," says the Lord of hosts,
"on the day that I make them my jewels."**

Malachi   3:17 NKJV

Oh My Daughter,

>I wish you could get even the smallest glimpse of my love for you. It would change everything in your life. You would stand taller, realizing your eternal destiny in me. You would rest easier, understanding my ever-present care for you. You would have unbounded hope, because you would finally understand that nothing is impossible for me—nothing! You would have joy just being in my presence as I have joy just being in yours.

So here's what I want you to do today: put down everything that's troubling you and come to me. Put your ear to my heart and listen. You will hear me saying that you are mine—my treasure and my jewel—and it's time for you to rest in me.

Your Loving Father,
>God

== == ==   == == == == == == == == ==

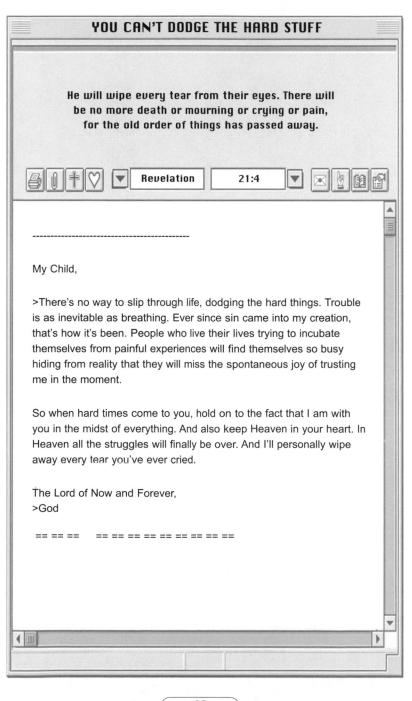

YOU CAN'T DODGE THE HARD STUFF

He will wipe every tear from their eyes. There will
be no more death or mourning or crying or pain,
for the old order of things has passed away.

Revelation 21:4

My Child,

>There's no way to slip through life, dodging the hard things. Trouble is as inevitable as breathing. Ever since sin came into my creation, that's how it's been. People who live their lives trying to incubate themselves from painful experiences will find themselves so busy hiding from reality that they will miss the spontaneous joy of trusting me in the moment.

So when hard times come to you, hold on to the fact that I am with you in the midst of everything. And also keep Heaven in your heart. In Heaven all the struggles will finally be over. And I'll personally wipe away every tear you've ever cried.

The Lord of Now and Forever,
>God

== == ==   == == == == == == == == ==

COME ON IN!

I no longer call you servants, because a servant
does not know his master's business. Instead,
I have called you friends, for everything that I
learned from my Father I have made known to you.

| John | 15:15 |

My Daughter,

>I'm not like some supernatural magician trying to hide the secret
of my tricks from you. I want you to know me and all the mysteries of
my kingdom. I want you to have access to my mind, my purposes,
my reasoning.

That's why I sent Jesus in human form to earth. He stepped out of the
mysteriously spiritual and into the humanly accessible. When you
found Him, you found the key to the mystery. He puts his arm around
you and brings you into my presence, saying, "Father, this woman is
a friend of mine and I'm vouching for her. She wants to know you." Do
you think I'd ever deny a request like that? No way!

Your Father and Friend,
>God

== == ==   == == == == == == == == ==

DON'T RUSH ME!

He who began a good work in you will carry it on to completion until the day of Christ Jesus.

| Philippians | 1:6 |

Dear Child of Mine,

>You are a masterpiece conceived in my heart, far more priceless than any painting or sculpture ever displayed in a museum. But you're an incomplete work of art. I'm still working on you, and I'm the kind of person who won't quit till the last brush stroke is perfect in my sight.

So don't rush me. Give me some space to work. And when you're tempted to give up on yourself, don't even think about it! I love what I've started in you, and I'm going to stay on the job until I'm 100 percent satisfied. Work with me. Trust me. You're going to love the finished product!

Your Creator,
>God

== == ==   == == == == == == == == ==

LOVE THEM FOR ME

If anyone says, "I love God," yet hates his brother, he is a liar. For anyone who does not love his brother, whom he has seen, cannot love God, whom he has not seen.

| | 1 John | | 4:20 | | |

My Daughter,

>Loving me was not an idea that just sprang into your head one day. I put it there. I loved you from the beginning so that you would love me and be my agent of love on earth. Because Jesus lives in you through the Holy Spirit, you can love others with his love.

Believe me, you could never "work up" a Jesus kind of love from the sweat of your own good intentions. But when you step back and let my Spirit do the loving through you, you'll find yourself caring for the most unusual people. Not only the attractive, witty, intelligent, lovable people, but all the beat-up, run-down, rag-tag brothers and sisters walking beside you on this difficult road called life. Take the love I have for you and love them for me.

The Ultimate Lover,
>God

== == ==   == == == == == == == == ==

DON'T DECIDE ALONE

Since ancient times no one has heard, no ear has perceived, no eye has seen any God besides you, who acts on behalf of those who wait for him.

Isaiah 64:4

My Daughter,

>I realize that your life often seems like an obstacle course of decisions needing to be made. Should you sell your car before it needs a brake job? Should you leave the job you detest, not knowing whether you'll find another one? Should you move to a new city or stay where you are?

I want you to know that you don't have to decide anything alone. I will be your confidant, your advisor, your friend in the midst of every hard decision. If you will share your problems with me, I will give you guidance and a sense of peace about what to do. So trust me and stay in touch, my child. I will act on your behalf.

Your Counselor,
>God

== == ==   == == == == == == == == ==

LET THEM CATCH YOU IN THE ACT

These commandments that I give you today are to be upon your hearts. Impress them on your children. Talk about them when you sit at home and when you walk along the road, when you lie down and when you get up.

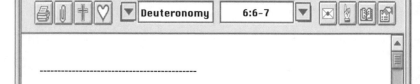

| Deuteronomy | 6:6-7 |

My Daughter,

>What are your kids learning today that they can keep as adults? What will they be able to hang on to from their formative years? I hope they'll remember times of love and laughter, seasons of blessing and struggle, bedtime prayers, evening meals, family celebrations.

But in the midst of it all, may their strongest memory be the faith they saw in you—your prayers for them, your words of encouragement, your loving commitment to me. May they see something so real and vibrant in you that it draws them to me. Every day let them catch you in the act of loving me. Nothing in this world will matter more when it comes to the formation of their own faith.

Your Father and Your Friend,
>God

== == ==   == == == == == == == == ==

CREATE A CHAIN REACTION

He . . . established the law in Israel, which he commanded
our forefathers to teach their children, so the next
generation would know them, even the children yet
to be born, and they in turn would tell their children.

Psalm 78:5-6

Dear Child,

>There's an old saying: "A chain is only as strong as its weakest link."
When I spoke my words of life to the people of Israel, I commissioned
them to create a chain of faith. I told them to teach their children my
words so that their children could teach the next generation. Each
succeeding generation was to become a link in this chain.

In the same way, your relationship with me is a link in your family's
chain of faith. It may be the very first link, or there may have been
many believers before you. But it's important to your children and
your grandchildren that you teach them well and show them my love.
Together we will keep your family's chain of faith strong for
generations to come.

The Forger of Your Chain,
>God

== == ==   == == == == == == == == ==

IF YOU SAY SO

"Sir," Simon Peter replied, "we worked hard all last night and didn't catch a thing. But if you say so, we'll try again."

| | Luke | 5:5 TLB | |

My Daughter,

>Has your practical knowledge of a situation ever gotten in the way of my spiritual guidance? It almost did in Peter's case. One night Peter had used all of his practical knowledge to catch fish, but he had returned to shore with an empty boat. Then Jesus suggested that he let down his nets in deeper water.

From a commonsense standpoint, Peter could have written off my Son's suggestion. But he heard an authority in Jesus' words that was more powerful than earthly expertise. So he responded, *"If you say so,* we'll try again." And this time Peter's nets were bulging with fish.

So don't rely solely on human wisdom, my child. Trust me when I call you into deeper waters. There you will find me and my answers.

Your Guide,
>God

== == ==   == == == == == == == == ==

WALK AS JESUS DID

He then began to teach them that the Son of Man must suffer many things and be rejected by the elders, chief priests and teachers of the law, and that he must be killed and after three days rise again.

Mark 8:31

Dear Child,

>Your faith journey will not be a Sunday stroll through the park. Far from it. You'll suffer problems and rejection just as everyone else does. But one of the most comforting and empowering things you can do is to remember that Jesus went through those same things. He was rejected, misunderstood, blamed, deserted, and betrayed. How did he live through it all without trying to hurt the ones who had hurt him? He relied totally on me.

As you grow in your faith, you'll learn to walk in the Spirit just as Jesus did—trusting me to see you through every challenge.

Your Traveling Companion,
>God

== == ==   == == == == == == == == ==

TRY AN ATTITUDE ADJUSTMENT

Your attitude should be the same as that of Christ Jesus: Who, being in very nature God, did not consider equality with God something to be grasped, but made himself nothing, taking the very nature of a servant, being made in human likeness.

| Philippians | 2:5-7 |

Dear Child,

>Am I really asking you to have an attitude like Jesus'? Yes, I am. "But he was God," you say. "I'm just a mom, barely surviving life in the diaper lane." Or, "I'm just a single woman working a forty-hour week." What's the connection?

The connection is humility. Jesus could have stayed in Heaven enjoying the praise of angels. Instead he voluntarily set aside his rights, humbly embracing my plan. You may look back on days when you got to sleep late, when you had more time for yourself. You may resent the diapers or the desk. But I'm asking you to set aside your rights and embrace your job with humility. You are where you are for my purposes.

Your Employer,
>God

LET MY SPIRIT PRAY THROUGH YOU

The Spirit helps us in our weakness. We do not know what
we ought to pray for, but the Spirit himself intercedes
for us with groans that words cannot express.

Romans **8:26**

Dear Child,

>Some days prayer is easy. The words flow out of you like a stream.
But other days when you feel distant from me, your prayer is more
like a stagnant pool. There are no words. What do you do in the
stagnant times? Keep praying. You see, I'm not up here in Heaven
answering only the smooth and beautiful prayers. I'm not impressed
with your eloquence.

In fact, it might surprise you to know that your power to pray does
not come from you at all. It's my gift of grace given to you through
my Holy Spirit. So open your heart and let my Spirit pray through
you, and your prayers will begin to flow again. I'm waiting to hear
from you.

The One Who Listens and Answers,
>God

== == ==   == == == == == == == == ==

YOUR FRIEND

[For my determined purpose is]
that I may know him.

Philippians **3:10 AMP**

My Daughter,

>Suppose you were asked to write an essay about your best friend.
Would you start by giving her physical stats (height, weight, hair color,
etc.)? Would you present a personal history (date and place of birth,
etc)? No. You would probably want to describe her zany sense of
humor, her loyalty, her unique talents—things like that.

Do you know Jesus as a friend, or is he just a character in a book? If
you know him more as a history lesson than a real person, your faith
is in trouble. Doctrine meant nothing to Mary Magdelene, but she
knew her Lord, and he was everything to her. Jesus yearns for that
kind of friendship with you. So do I.

Your Father and Friend,
>God

== == ==   == == == == == == == == ==

HIGH OCTANE PRAISE

**I will praise you, O Lord, with all my heart;
I will tell of all your wonders.**

| Psalm | 9:1 |

Dear Child,

>Life requires a full tank of energy. Some days the engine of your enthusiasm sputters and dies, and you feel like you're running on fumes. Let me give you a high-octane remedy that will refuel your tank and kick your heart back into gear. That remedy is praise.

Start by praising me for whatever is going on. "Lord, I praise you for this teething baby, this messy desk, this pile of laundry. Lord, I praise you that you're in control of all these things, and you're with me in the midst of them." Then begin to praise me for my wonders, my blessings, my presence, my mercy. Sing to me. Give me your heart. You'll be amazed at the refreshing power that will fill you.

The Fuel in Your Spiritual Tank,
>God

== == ==   == == == == == == == == ==

THE REAL ISSUE

They found the stone rolled away from the tomb. Then they went in and did not find the body of the Lord Jesus.

Luke   24:2-3 NKJV

My Child,

>I assume you've found out by now that there will be some bad times in your life. The real issue is not whether you'll have bad times, but whether you'll trust me to bring good out of those bad times. The real issue is not whether your life will be hard, but whether you're willing to keep loving me and living for my purposes even in the hard times.

Remember, Jesus triumphed over Satan on the third day, not the first. Your challenge is to believe the third day is coming even when you feel as if you're stuck in the tomb. Keep believing in me and trusting in my power to redeem, and you will rise up from the tomb of your troubles.

Your Resurrection Power,
>God

== == ==   == == == == == == == == ==

THE RIGHT PLACE AT THE RIGHT TIME

Anna, a prophetess . . . did not depart from the temple, but served God with fastings and prayers night and day.

| | | | ▼ | Luke | 2:36-37 NKJV | ▼ | | | | |

My Daughter,

Anna was an old woman by the time Jesus was born. She had heard of the Messiah all her life, but so had every other Jew. Why was Anna the one who got to see him so soon after his birth? Why was she given the honor of proclaiming his birth to others in Israel? Because Anna was in the temple when Jesus was brought in to be dedicated.

But it was hardly a chance meeting. You see, Anna had been there, right where I wanted her, every day and night for seventy-seven years! She was in the right place at the right time to meet her Lord. Are you where I want you to be today? Every day is a good day for a holy encounter.

The One Who Meets You,
>God

== == ==   == == == == == == == == ==

ENTER IN

The LORD is the portion of my inheritance and my cup; You support my lot. The lines have fallen to me in pleasant places; Indeed, my heritage is beautiful to me.

Psalm 16:5-6 NASB

My Daughter,

>What if you were the heir to a great fortune and your father were holding a huge banquet in your honor where he planned to give you your inheritance? The tables were set. Delicious food had been prepared. Your father was waiting proudly for you to walk through the door. Would you sit at the gates of your father's house and not enter because you felt he didn't love you?

Sadly, this is true of many of my children. They sit at the gates of their inheritance thinking I don't love them, believing instead that I am here only to keep track of their sins and make them pay in the end.

Everything is set, my daughter. The guests have arrived. I am proudly waiting for you to walk through the door of my acceptance. You are my child in whom I am well pleased. Enter in.

Your Proud Father,
>God

== == ==   == == == == == == == == ==

HIRE THE RIGHT ARCHITECT

**Unless the Lord builds the house,
its builders labor in vain.**

| Psalm | 127:1 |

Dear Child,

>Have you ever experienced the excitement of building a new
home—drawing the plans, hiring the workmen, choosing the
materials, and then watching it become all that you envisioned?

Here's something to keep in mind as you create your dream house.
All of your labor and creativity will be wasted if I am not involved. If
my Spirit is not the power behind every decision, if my love is not the
force that motivates each choice, the house may be beautiful, but it
will lack the warmth required to make it a real home. So let me help
you plan and build and decorate your house. Then invite me to live
there with you. I am the one who can make your house a home.

Your Architect,
>God

== == ==   == == == == == == == == ==

MEANING IN YOUR MOMENTS

**Teach us to number our days aright,
that we may gain a heart of wisdom.**

Psalm	90:12

Dear Child,

>Every year a new beginning stretches out before you. You buy a new calendar with empty pages. Then week by week, month by month, you fill it with appointments and activities. You rush in this direction and that, and all the while, your life is slipping through your fingers like sand through an hourglass.

Have you ever stopped to think that every minute is an original. Once it is gone, there will be no instant replays. To "number your days aright" is not merely to get your schedule in order. It is to measure the meaning in your moments. Are you just rushing around, or are you taking the time to enjoy the life I've given you?

The Meaning in Each Moment,
>God

== == ==   == == == == == == == == ==

SHOW AND TELL

Tell your children and grandchildren how I . . .
performed my signs among them . . .
that you may know that I am the Lord.

| Exodus | 10:2 |

My Daughter,

>There's nothing like an example of my power and mercy to make a believer out of a doubter. It's one thing to say to your child, "God is love." It's quite another to say, "Remember when Daddy lost his job? We prayed, and God led Daddy to a new job." Or, "When I was a little girl your age, we moved to a new town, and I was so lonely. But Jesus helped me make new friends." Those are real, personal examples that will help your child put a face on my love.

Keep a notebook of answered prayers and share them with your children. Then don't be surprised if they begin keeping their own notebook of blessings.

The One Who Loves,
>God

== == ==   == == == == == == == == ==

YOU'RE BURSTING WITH CREATIVITY

**I will praise You, for I am fearfully
and wonderfully made.**

Psalm **139:14 NKJV**

Dear Child,

>I want you to see my creative genius not only in the natural world but also in the incredible diversity of my children. Every person is created so uniquely that not one is exactly like another. Every fingerprint on every hand on every person in every land is different. Think about it. I delighted to give each of you a special identity, yet many people spend their whole lives trying to blend in.

Don't deny your uniqueness by trying to play out the colorful human drama in blacks and whites. Don't ignore the brush strokes of my creativity. And never forget that you are created in my image. You are wonderfully made, bursting with amazing creativity of your own.

Your Great Creator,
>God

== == ==   == == == == == == == == ==

LET'S WORK ON OUR FRIENDSHIP

The friend who attends the bridegroom waits and listens for him, and is full of joy when he hears the bridegroom's voice. That joy is mine, and it is now complete.

John   3:29

My Daughter,

>Has it ever occurred to you that sometimes you treat me more like a vending machine than a friend? When you meet with me, you begin by stuffing your prayer requests into my hands, like quarters in a slot, so I'll dispense what you need.

Suppose you met one of your other friends for lunch and treated her that way. Before you even said hello, you started telling her everything you wanted her to do for you—drive your carpool, pick up your laundry, and so on. She might feel a little bit put down.

You and I are friends, my daughter. Can't we have a little visit before you give me my "to do" list? There's so much I want to share with you.

Your Father,
>God

== == ==   == == == == == == == == ==

CHOOSE HEALTHY THOUGHTS

To be carnally minded is death; but to be spiritually minded is life and peace.

Romans 8:6 KJV

My Child,

>Picture your mind as a grocery cart. You can fill it with whatever you choose. You can roll it down filthy alleyways lined with garbage cans, filling it with rotting leftovers, if that's your choice. But if you visit the clean, bright aisles of your favorite grocery store, choosing fresh vegetables and fruit, lean meats, and fresh breads, your body and your taste buds will thank you for it.

Just as foods determine the health of your body, your thoughts determine the health of your mind and spirit. So don't load up on envy or pride or lust. Choose healthy thoughts that bring life and peace.

Your Grocer,
>God

== == ==   == == == == == == == == ==

COME HOME AND COME CLEAN

**Create in me a clean heart, O God; and
renew a steadfast spirit within me.**

| Psalm | 51:10 KJV |

My Child,

>I run the only quality cleaning business for the children I love. When you fall and fail, don't stay camped out in a pigpen of remorse. Whether your soul is slightly soiled or majorly filthy, bring it in to me. Show me where the dirt is, and I'll go to work. I'll forgive what needs to be forgiven and give you a new heart—a clean heart that's full of hope for the future. I'll renew your dreams, your visions, and your goals and give you the strength you'll need to make a new beginning. So come home, come clean, and start fresh. I'm ready if you are!

The Heart Cleaner,
>God

== == ==   == == == == == == == == ==

GUARD YOUR GARDEN WELL

**Above all else, guard your heart,
for it is the wellspring of life.**

| Proverbs | 4:23 |

My Daughter,

>Suppose you planted a beautiful vegetable garden. Tender lettuce, crisp parsley, ripening tomatoes are all ready to harvest. But on the day you decided to make your first, fresh, homegrown salad, you walked out to discover a family of rabbits making a meal out of your vegetables. Wouldn't you build a fence to keep them out?

Your heart is like that garden. All that is healthy and life-giving is meant to grow and flourish there. But if you don't build a protective shield around it, it will be open to every kind of intruder, and the harvest of your heart will be vulnerable to destruction. So guard the garden of your heart with a fence of my truth.

The Lord of the Harvest,
>God

== == ==   == == == == == == == == ==

ONE-ON-ONE TIME

**I call on you, O God, for you will answer me;
give ear to me and hear my prayer.**

Psalm 17:6

My Child,

>Have you ever noticed a child in a grocery store trying to get his mother's attention? "Mama? Mama?" he'll say. But Mama's mind is a million miles away. "Mom?" he'll persist. Still no answer.

Earthly parents can sometimes tune out, but I'm not like that. I'm always tuned in, so when you call, I hear you. When you need some one-on-one time, I'm available. I'm the Friend who listens and cares and the Father who waits to hear your voice. So don't hold back. Come to me today. I'm ready to listen. And you know what? If *you're* ready to hear me, I'll speak to your heart.

Your Friend and Father,
>God

== == ==   == == == == == == == == ==

FOR THE JOY

**Keep your eyes on Jesus, our leader and instructor.
He was willing to die a shameful death on the cross
because of the joy he knew would be his afterwards; and
now he sits in the place of honor by the throne of God.**

Hebrews 12:2 TLB

My Child,

>How was Jesus able to go through the unspeakable horror of the crucifixion—the travesty of justice, the mockery and cruelty? How was he able to lift the cross onto his beaten and bloody shoulders and walk the Way of Sorrows, knowing full well where it led? How was he able to take the nails in his hands and feet, the hours of torture, and the spear in his side? And worst by far, how was he able to go through it all, feeling totally forsaken by me?

He was able to do it all because he knew the joy that lay ahead of him—the joy of extending his grace and love to you and then living with you forever in my kingdom. That's how and why he did all that he did—because of the joy.

His Father and Yours,
>God

== == ==   == == == == == == == == ==

IT'S YOUR CALL

**Call to me and I will answer you and tell you
great and unsearchable things you do not know.**

| 🖨 📎 ✝ ♡ ▼ | Jeremiah | 33:3 | ▼ ✉ ✋ 📖 🗒 |

Oh My Child,

>Have you ever wondered why I created you? I created you to be in relationship with me. I want to share everything with you: my amazing vision, my far-reaching wisdom that is broader and deeper and higher than you can imagine, the unsearchable wonders of my heart.

But I don't want to force these things on you. I'm waiting for you to want what I'm offering. Just call out to me. Make the slightest move in my direction, and I'll meet you there. Believe me, what I have for you is something you don't want to miss. But it's your call.

The GIft-gIver,
>God

== == ==   == == == == == == == == ==

BE A WISE INVESTER

If you call out for insight and cry aloud for understanding, and if you look for it as for silver and search for it as for hidden treasure, then you will understand the fear of the LORD and find the knowledge of God.

Proverbs 2:3-5

My Daughter,

>Look around you. So many people are clamoring for money, possessions, position, and prestige. Those things are so transient. Money can be lost. Possessions wear out and go out of style. Position and prestige are fleeting prizes in life's tug-of-war.

Search instead for spiritual understanding. It brings knowledge of me, a reverence for my Son, and an awe of my Holy Spirit. These are the things that make a woman truly wealthy—wealthy in wisdom, serenity, hope, and joy. Can you think of any stock on the stock market that guarantees that kind of dividend? Be a wise investor, my daughter. Invest in understanding.

Your Loving Father,
>God

== == ==   == == == == == == == == ==

THE GROWTH PRINCIPLE

Do not be deceived: God cannot be mocked. A man reaps
what he sows. The one who sows to please his sinful nature,
from that nature will reap destruction; the one who sows
to please the Spirit, from the Spirit will reap eternal life.

| | | Galatians | | 6:7-8 | | | |

Dear Child,

>You don't have to be raised on a farm to know that if you want to
raise corn, you don't plant turnips. Whatever you put in the ground
will come out of the ground. That's how it works.

Well, exactly the same principle operates in the spiritual realm. If you
plant dishonesty, jealousy, lust, envy, and gossip, the crop you reap
will damage and destroy not only you but your loved ones as well. But
if you purposely set out to plant love, faith, gentleness, encouragement,
and grace, the yield of your life will amaze you. You will harvest an
abundant life that lasts forever.

Your Father,
>God

== == ==   == == == == == == == == ==

ANY OLD CRACKED POT WILL DO!

We have this treasure in earthen vessels, that the excellency of the power may be of God, and not of us.

| 2 Corinthians | 4:7 KJV |

Dearest Daughter,

>When the waitress sets a jug of pure maple syrup on the table in your favorite pancake restaurant, are you thinking about the jug? Not really. Instead, you probably can't wait to pour syrup on a stack of warm, buttery pancakes.

What's my point here? You are the jug in this little analogy, and my Holy Spirit is the syrup. I created you as a container to hold and dispense my amazing Spirit of love in the world. Nothing delights me more than filling the people I've created with my power. And the good news is this: it doesn't take an exquisite porcelain pitcher to contain my Spirit. Any old cracked pot will do! So let my Spirit make himself at home in you, and before long I'll be using your life to pour out my love on everyone around you.

The Spirit-giver,
>God

== == ==   == == == == == == == == ==

A SEED OF ETERNITY

He has also set eternity in the hearts of men; yet they cannot fathom what God has done from beginning to end.

| | Ecclesiastes | 3:11 | |

My Daughter,

>The day I created you, I planted a tiny seed in your heart. That seed contains the potential for eternal life with me. It will either grow or wither, depending on how you live your life. If you choose to focus all of your time, talent, love, and attention on the visible, tangible, temporal things around you, the seed of eternal life will wither. But if you nourish it by focusing on the invisible, intangible but lasting things of my kingdom, it will grow.

If you invest your heart in getting to know me, if you water that tiny seed with faith and prayer, you will be able to watch it flourish, growing up into a mighty tree that brings shade and shelter to all who find it. Your daily choices will make the difference in your growth.

Your Everlasting Father,
>God

== == ==   == == == == == == == == ==

UNDER THE CIRCUMSTANCES

**Be joyful in hope, patient in affliction,
faithful in prayer.**

Romans 12:12

Dear Child,

>Have you ever asked a friend how she was doing and heard her
reply, "Pretty good, under the circumstances"? There's no need for
you to live "under the circumstances." I've given you a gift that will
free you from the circumstantial undertow. That gift is prayer.

Prayer unlocks the door of hopelessness and releases you into hope.
Prayer admits you into my presence, where we can fellowship as
friends. Prayer invites unexpected joy into seasons of sorrow. In
prayer you'll find the patience to persevere in troubles. You'll learn to
trust my will even when you don't understand it. You'll find peace that
passes understanding in times of conflict. So come to me in prayer. I'll
lift you over your circumstances.

The One Who Meets You,
>God

== == ==   == == == == == == == == ==

WILLING TO BE WILLING

Now the Lord came and stood and called as at other times, "Samuel! Samuel!" And Samuel answered, "Speak, for Your servant hears."

| 1 Samuel | 3:10 NKJV |

My Daughter,

>Suppose you had two cars. One was shiny and beautiful, but when you turned the key the engine didn't run. The other car was small and slow, but when you turned the key, the engine cranked right up. Which car would you use? Obviously, you'd use the smaller, slower car.

This is a picture of why I replaced Eli, the older, more experienced prophet, with Samuel, who was just a little boy. Eli had begun to get weary and jaded. He allowed sinful practices in my temple, and he didn't listen to me. But little Samuel would rise out of a sound sleep every time I called his name, and he would do whatever I asked of him. Samuel was not sophisticated, but he was willing to be used. My child, if you're willing to be willing, there's no limit to what I can do in your life.

Your Father,
>God

== == ==   == == == == == == == == ==

WHAT LEGACY WILL YOU LEAVE?

Lord, help me to realize how brief my time on earth will be. Help me know that I am here but for a moment more.

Psalm	39:4 TLB

My Dear Child,

>Do you realize how brief a lifetime really is? Even people who live to be a hundred have only been around for the blink of an eye when compared to eternity. Considering the brevity of your own lifetime, shouldn't you do some thinking about how you'll use it? What will it amount to? What kind of legacy will you leave? Will you focus mostly on yourself, or will you bless others? Will you be driven by selfish desires, or will you follow my lead and work for my purposes?

There is always more beauty and peace and purpose in the life of a woman who has lived for me and loved others than there is in the life of one who has lived selfishly. Choose now to leave a legacy of love.

The Love of a Lifetime,
>God

== == ==   == == == == == == == == ==

BE FEARLESS!

The Lord is my helper; I will not be afraid. What can man do to me?

Hebrews 13:6

My Daughter,

Suppose I asked you to list your top three fears. Would you list failure, success, the opinion of others? Now suppose I asked you to give me that little list of fears and let me throw it into my fire of love. Would you trust me enough to do it?

Living in fear is like handing over your house key to a thief and inviting him to rob you blind. Fear can rob you of hope, joy, and your sense of adventure. It can even rob you of your destiny. I want you to live fearlessly—to follow the dreams I have set in you, to be true to the gifts and abilities that are uniquely yours. Let me burn that list of fears. Be free! Be fearless!

The Lord of the Adventure,
>God

== == ==   == == == == == == == == ==

A FIELD TRIP

I am the Lord your God, who teaches you what is best for you, who directs you in the way you should go.

| Isaiah | 48:17 |

My Child,

>When you were in school, who was your favorite teacher? Was she the one who read out of the textbook in a monotone so boring that you could hardly stay awake? Or was she the teacher who breathed excitement into her lessons by relating them to real life?

The Christian journey is not a boring classroom. It has nothing to do with hiding behind a desk. I am the Teacher who takes you out into the thick of life's real adventures. At every crossroads, I know which turn you should take. At every point of indecision, I know which choice you should make. Begin to see each new day with me as a kind of field trip in which I'll teach you something new as we walk together.

Your Teacher,
>God

== == ==   == == == == == == == == ==

SERENITY IS POSSIBLE

All his busy rushing ends in nothing.

	Psalm	93:5 TLB	

My Child,

>Have you ever watched a hamster running around and around on his little plastic wheel? He actually thinks he's getting somewhere. Do you ever feel like that—rushing around, hurrying, worrying, ending the day exhausted, and wondering if you've gotten anywhere?

I want to help you stop the stress. I want to help you live as peacefully as a little child in her Father's house. Is that possible? It is! Even though your circumstances may not change, I can change *you* within those circumstances.

Make prayer your first priority. Let me help you order your day. Then let me work and shop and ride beside you during each commitment, and the serenity you yearn for will become a reality.

The Quiet Center of Who You Are,
>God

== == ==   == == == == == == == == ==

WHAT THEY SEE IS WHAT THEY DO

**Train a child in the way he should go, and
when he is old he will not turn from it.**

| Proverbs | 22:6 |

My Daughter,

>A well-known family counselor once said, "Most problems in children
are the reflection of what lies in the hearts of their parents." This is
why telling your children to practice what you don't practice is pretty
pointless. Telling them to refrain from what you do practice is a waste
of words.

Children, from a very early age, are parent-watchers and imitators.
What they see is what they do. So your job as a parent is, first, to
become the kind of person you would desire your child to be. Only
then will you have earned the right to instruct. Surrender your heart to
me, and my Spirit will make you the parent you need to be.

Your Loving Parent,
>God

== == ==   == == == == == == == == ==

RECEIVING IS ALSO A BLESSING

It is more blessed to give than to receive.

| Acts | 20:35 |

My Daughter,

>You have heard my saying, "It is more blessed to give than to receive." But do you know that receiving is also a blessing? To show your neediness is to open the arms of your spirit to the intimacy of friendship. To receive help from a person who reaches out to meet your needs is to welcome a transaction of love.

If you ever expect to live in a love relationship with me, you'd better get used to receiving because I am constantly giving gifts and meeting needs. Faith in me is never an independent, do-it-yourself kind of life. So receive all that I have for you, my daughter.

The Gift and the Giver,
>God

== == ==   == == == == == == == == ==

DON'T RUN FROM YOUR DESTINY

**Where can I go from your Spirit?
Where can I flee from your presence?**

| Psalm | 139:7 |

Dear Daughter,

>Do you love to travel—to book your tickets, pack your bags, and leave everything behind? Well, there's one thing you can never leave behind: me and my love. No matter how far you go, I'll be there, continually drawing you to me, continually speaking to you and urging you to let me have a say in your life.

Sure, you can go your own way and make your own plans, but what you try to run from will follow and find you. The call you didn't want to hear in church you'll hear in a conversation or read in the newspaper. The destiny you turned your back on will meet you around every corner. So, don't run away, my daughter. Your life's true meaning and your heart's deep contentment are found in me.

Your Destiny,
>God

== == ==   == == == == == == == == ==

THE SWEETEST WORK YOU'LL EVER DO

**Let the beauty of the Lord our God be upon us,
and establish the work of our hands for us.**

Psalm 90:17 NKJV

Dear Child of Mine,

>Sometimes the world looks down on a woman who doesn't hold a job with pay. But I want you to know that whether you work outside the home or not, some of the sweetest work you will ever do is serving your family. When it's done in the right spirit, caring for those you love is a blessing to them and to you.

Because serving others was one of my Son's highest priorities, you'll feel his nearness in a special way when you're serving your family members. Whether you're polishing a tabletop or tossing a salad or reading a story to a child, you are in the process of creating a haven of beauty and welcome for the ones you love. So embrace each small act of service as a sacrifice of praise.

The Heart of Your Home,
>God

== == ==   == == == == == == == == ==

WHAT'S "IN" MAY SOON BE OUT

Charm is deceptive, and beauty is fleeting; but a woman who fears the Lord is to be praised.

| Proverbs | 31:30 |

My Daughter,

>Every season fashion magazines come out with issues featuring the creations of famous designers. Many people go into a spending frenzy making sure their closets contain that "in look" even though what's in now may be out in a year or less. There is nothing wrong with wanting to look good. But make sure you understand the fickle, fleeting nature of outer beauty.

I'm looking for inner beauty—for a radiant heart that stands in awe of me and longs to please me. When I see a woman with a heart like that, I say to myself, "What a beauty!" So, my daughter, be sure you spend more time reading my Book on inner beauty than reading magazines on outer fashions. Humility and faith never go out of style.

The One Who Knows True Beauty,
>God

== == ==   == == == == == == == == ==

THE DUCKLING'S STRENGTH

**I am well content with weaknesses, with insults,
with distresses, with persecutions, with difficulties,
for Christ's sake; for when I am weak, then I am strong.**

| | | | | | 2 Corinthians | 12:10 NASB | | | | | |

My Daughter,

>Remember the story of the ugly duckling? He was a swan born by accident into a duck family. He grew up feeling sad and incredibly different. But it was that very difference that eventually matured him into a beautiful adult swan.

Sometimes the characteristic or weakness that you have hated about yourself can become the very thing that blesses you the most.

In our relationship, that's true of all of your weaknesses. That's because your weaknesses make you cry out for my strength. That's when your weakness becomes a blessing rather than a curse. It is the very thing that leads you into my arms. So glory in your weaknesses. Let them lead you to my strength.

Your Strength,
>God

== == == == == == == == == == ==

NO LAUGHING MATTER

Lot went out and spoke to his sons-in-law, who were to marry his daughters, and said, "Up, get out of this place, for the LORD will destroy the city."

Genesis 19:14 NASB

My Daughter,

>The movies have created a stereotype of a Christian doomsayer foaming at the mouth and wearing an apocalyptic message on a billboard. This type of character is meant to be comical in the movies.

But believe me, sin and its effects are no laughing matter. So when you hear me saying, "Get out of this place; it's going to be the death of you," you can be sure I'm serious. Because I love you, I will never allow you to die in your sin without giving you a warning message and providing a way out. But it's important for you to react quickly, or you may suffer real (even deadly) consequences. Repent and get out of "Sinsville."

The One Who Provides a Way Out,
>God

== == ==   == == == == == == == == ==

FORGET THE NEW-FANGLED BRANDS

These nations, which you are about to dispossess,
give heed to soothsayers and to diviners; but as for
you, the Lord your God has not allowed you so to do.

Deuteronomy 18:14 RSV

My Daughter,

>Some people these days think Christianity is out of style. They see it as a worn-out sofa in an old junk shop. "A more culturally relative belief is available at Faith-Mart around the corner," they seem to imply. "In fact, why would you want to worship God when we could set it up for you to *be* God?"

The problem with the Faith-Mart brands is that there is no redemption, no solid foundation, no absolute truth. Practicing these new-fangled faiths is like painting your portrait in the rain. It doesn't last. But following me is like sculpting a perfect you in priceless marble. You are so valuable to me, my daughter. Don't buy into the cheaper faiths.

The Genuine Article,
>God

== == ==   == == == == == == == == ==

YOU'RE MY CHOSEN ONE

The LORD said unto Samuel, Look not on his countenance . . . for the LORD seeth not as man seeth; for man looketh on the outward appearance, but the LORD looketh on the heart.

| 1 Samuel | 16: 7 KJV |

My Daughter,

>I am always on the lookout for the man or woman who is determined to follow me. I sent Samuel to Jesse's house, telling him to bring back the son of Jesse who was most intent on following me. Samuel considered every one of Jesse's adult sons, but couldn't find what I was looking for. Why?

The one I had set my heart on was the one who had set his heart on me, and he was only a boy. David had the humble, faithful, absolutely yielded spirit I was looking for.

Today my favor and love rest on you, my daughter. No matter what your shortcomings are, you are my chosen one. If you'll yield your heart totally to me, I'll use you in powerful ways. Will you be a woman after my own heart?

The One Who Looks Within,
>God

== == ==   == == == == == == == == ==

MOVE TOWARD THE PROMISE

I am confident of this very thing, that He who began a good work in you will perfect it until the day of Christ Jesus.

Philippians 1:6 NASB

My Daughter,

>Everyone knows that caterpillars turn into butterflies eventually. But they are definitely caterpillars first. They can't fly; they move slowly; and they look like big, fat worms.

When you start your spiritual walk with me, I give you the promise of spiritual maturity, healing, and wholeness. But you aren't there yet. You are still a spiritual caterpillar. So stop beating yourself up for not being perfect and just keep moving toward the promise. I've created you to fly, but it is a process that takes time, patience, and lots of grace.

In fact, no one ever truly comes into the fullness of my promises until they pass through the cocoon of death into my perfect kingdom. So live graciously in this caterpillar state, being the woman I've created you to be. And keep moving toward the promise of flight.

Your Creator,
>God

== == ==   == == == == == == == == ==

YOU'RE ENTITLED

Having chosen us, he called us to come to him; and when we came, he declared us "not guilty," filled us with Christ's goodness, gave us right standing with himself, and promised us his glory.

Romans   **8:30** TLB

My Daughter,

>If your family owned a huge corporation, you wouldn't go into business headquarters every day and mop the floor, hoping to get some sort of paycheck. You would know your own sense of entitlement, security, and acceptance within that company.

Unfortunately, there are children of mine who already have the full inheritance of my kingdom but still feel a need to earn a place in the company. They're still mopping up outside my heart, trying to earn what is already theirs. Your good deeds shouldn't be done to earn my acceptance. You already have all of my love. Receive your place in my corporation.

Your Father,
>God

== == == == == == == == == == == ==

COME AS YOU ARE

**God demonstrates His own love toward us, in that
while we were yet sinners, Christ died for us.**

Romans   5:8 NASB

My Daughter,

>What if your son ran away and you searched high and low for him?
You dreamed about him at night and prayed every day for his return.
At last, one day you saw him coming down your driveway, beat up
and dirty. Would you say to him, "I'm sorry, son; it's good to see you
and all, but you'll have to go take a shower and get a job so you can
buy some new clothes. Then maybe you can come home"? I don't
think so! You'd run and embrace him and weep tears of joy. You'd run
a bath for him and nurse him back to health.

In the same way, you don't have to clean up before you come to me.
You are my child. No amount of dirt can keep you from my embrace.
No wound is too deep for my healing. Come as you are.

Your Father,
>God

== == ==   == == == == == == == == ==

NEVER GIVE UP

Your watchmen shall lift up their voices, with their voices they shall sing together; for they shall see eye to eye when the Lord brings back Zion.

Isaiah 52:8 NKJV

My Daughter,

>Family members of a relative who is MIA (missing and unaccounted for in military action) don't forget their missing family member as though he or she were dead. Many relatives even hang MIA flags outside their homes to symbolize their inability to give up on the missing soldiers. Many times they spend all of their money to find them and bring them home again.

That's how it should be for you as a Christian when you see Christian brothers or sisters fall away from the faith. Never give up on them. Seek them out lovingly. As long as they live, their spirits will long to return home; and as long as you live, your faith should hope and pray for their return. So hang a flag out for the spiritually missing in action and help them come home to me.

The One Who Waits,
>God

== == ==   == == == == == == == == ==

DON'T COME TO WATCH

You shall love the Lord your God with all your heart, and with all your soul, and with all your strength, and with all your mind.

| Luke | 10:27 NASB |

My Daughter,

>When you go to see a sporting event, all you have to do is buy a ticket. You can also choose to buy assorted foods that give you heartburn, but these things would have no effect on the game.

The worship experience is different. Showing up is only the beginning. The two main players on the field of worship are you and me. Though it may seem that the pastor and the worship leader are the main players, they're not. They know they are mainly there to encourage my meeting with you. So come with your heart right and ready to go. Give me 110 percent of your worship. Pray like you mean it. Wrestle with me about hard things. Seek me with all your heart. Worship is not a spectator sport, so don't come to watch. Come to play!

I'll meet you on the field,
>God

== == ==   == == == == == == == == ==

DON'T GIVE UP!

**Let us not get tired of doing what is right,
for after a while we will reap a harvest of
blessing if we don't get discouraged and give up.**

| 🖨 📎 ✝ ♡ ▼ | Galatians | 6:9 TLB | ▼ ✉ ✍ 📖 |

Dear Child,

>If you were to look for the common thread in most human success stories, you would find the thread of persistence. Each successful person, from Thomas Edison to Madam Curie to Beverly Sills, refused to let setbacks derail his or her ultimate goal. Regardless of roadblocks, successful people find a way to move forward.

This quality of persistence is even more vital in my kingdom. When I give you a job to do or a situation to pray about, I want you to refuse to be derailed by discouragement. Quitting assures defeat. And remember, it's not your power that will pull you through, but mine. "Not by might, not by power, but by my Spirit," says the Lord of Hosts.

Your Power to Persevere,
>God

== == ==   == == == == == == == == ==

SELF-MADE WOMEN WERE NOT MY IDEA

**I can do everything through him
who gives me strength.**

Philippians **4:13**

Child of Mine,

>If you really think you can hold the whole world up on your
shoulders, you're in for a dose of reality. If you really believe you're
mentally able to solve every problem life will throw at you, you're in
for a shock. You were never meant to depend on your own strength
or brain power. Self-made men and women were not my idea.

David was in touch with the source of his strength from an early age.
When all Israel was cowering in fear of a Philistine giant, David faced
Goliath with a slingshot and these words: "I come to you in the name
of the Lord. . . . This day [He] will deliver you into my hand." And I did.
So trust me in each situation, and I'll give you the strength you need
to face down every giant in your life.

The Source of Your Strength,
>God

== == ==   == == == == == == == == ==

GET RADICAL

Never be lacking in zeal, but keep your spiritual fervor, serving the Lord.

Romans	12:11

My Daughter,

>On a cold night, have you ever been looking forward to a bowl of hot soup only to find that it had cooled off? Bummer. Jesus feels the same way about his followers. He warned the Christians at Laodicea that if they didn't turn up the heat on their faith, he was going to spit them out like a mouthful of lukewarm soup.

Jesus has a love for you that is anything but lukewarm. He loves you so radically, he gave his life for you. He yearns for you to be passionate, radical, and sold out to him. He wants people to know that you're "on fire for the Lord." It's going to take that kind of fired-up spirit to stand against everything that will conspire to pull you off course on your Christian walk. So live passionately for my Son and for me.

Your Radical Father,
>God

== == ==   == == == == == == == == ==

A TRULY GOOD WIFE

If you can find a truly good wife, she is worth more than precious gems! Her husband can trust her, and she will richly satisfy his needs.

Proverbs 31:10-11 TLB

My Daughter,

>What is a truly good wife? I could use a lot of fifty-cent words to describe one, but I'll just put it simply. A truly good wife is one who chooses to act in the best interest of her husband. Her trustworthiness goes beyond simple marital fidelity to smaller issues, such as respecting the privacy of their marriage and staying within the family budget. She knows when her husband needs encouragement, and she gives it generously. She prays for him daily.

Loving like this is a choice she freely makes. It's a choice to honor him in word and deed—in the big things that show and in the small things he may not even notice.

The Inventor of Marriage,
>God

== == ==   == == == == == == == == ==

CONSIDER YOUR WORDS

**When words are many, sin is not absent,
but he who holds his tongue is wise.**

| Proverbs | 10:19 |

My Child,

>Words are powerful. They can build up or tear down, create harmony or chaos, introduce hope or despair. The woman who controls her tongue knows when to speak and when to be quiet. She doesn't always have to have the last word in every situation.

I know you have heard the term "holding your peace." You can do that, quite literally, when you control your tongue. Many times if you will wait and let me show you a better time, I'll open up an opportunity for you to speak your opinion in a nondestructive way. Let me give you the spirit of wisdom and patience, and your words can be instruments of peace at home and on the job.

The Living Word,
>God

== == ==   == == == == == == == == ==

GET OFF THAT RESTLESS ROAD

**Keep your lives free from the love of money and be
content with what you have, because God has said,
"Never will I leave you; never will I forsake you."**

Hebrews 13:5

My Child,

>Look around you. There are very few contented people. In the
business world men and women scramble for higher salaries, all the
while getting deeper in debt. The whole advertising industry centers
on influencing people to want what they do not need and desire what
they cannot afford.

I want to set you free from the lie that says one more item will satisfy
you. It won't. The truth is, one more item will only increase your desire
for yet another item. The world holds out an illusion of contentment
that drives you on like the carrot on a stick that drives the donkey
forward. Get off that restless road. The only true contentment you will
ever know is found in me. I am more than enough.

Your Contentment,
>God

== == ==   == == == == == == == == ==

THE FAITH-LIFE IS NOT A SHOW

**I will be careful to lead a blameless life. . . .
I will walk in my house with a blameless heart.**

Psalm 101:2

My Daughter,

>Have you ever watched an impressive Christian speaker handle my Word before a crowd? *What a spiritual superstar!* you may have thought. That speaker may have gifts, and she may use them well in public, but the crowds never see her at home. What is she like with her husband? Is she encouraging and tender? What is she like with her children? Does she take time to listen and help with their problems? What kind of neighbor is she? What kind of friend?

My child, this life of faith is not a show. I am far more interested in who you are when the spotlight's turned off and the crowd goes home. I want to help you live blamelessly on the stage of everyday life among those who know you best.

The Lord Who Knows You,
>God

== == ==   == == == == == == == == ==

I'VE SEEN IT ALL!

Because of the Lord's great love we are not consumed, for his compassions never fail. They are new every morning; great is your faithfulness.

| | Lamentations | 3:22-23 | | |

My Daughter,

>Don't ever think that you've blown it so badly there's no starting over. Just when you think your sin has killed my grace, my mercies spring up like flowers in a flower bed. If I had to make up a nickname for myself it would be "The God of New Beginnings" because helping you start over is my specialty.

If you don't believe me, read the Bible. It is, quite simply, a history of people's messing up and my cleaning up. Flawed and sinful men and women are on every page. Name a sin, and it's in there.

Believe me, whatever wrong you've done saddens me because it hurts you, but it doesn't surprise me. I've seen it all. So don't stay away. I've got plenty of forgiveness with your name on it.

The Faithful One,
>God

== == ==   == == == == == == == == ==

MY DEFINITION OF BEAUTY

Your beauty should not come from outward adornment, such as braided hair and the wearing of gold jewelry and fine clothes. Instead, it should be that of your inner self, the unfading beauty of a gentle and quiet spirit, which is of great worth in God's sight.

| | 1 Peter | 3:3-4 | |

My Daughter,

>What makes a great beauty? The fashion industry has one point of view, and I have another. Designers in the garment trade find a waiflike woman's body and use it as a coat hanger on which to hang their designs. They teach it to tramp up and down a runway and pose for the camera. And they call it beautiful. They find a face with attractive features, and they make it up until it's hard to recognize the person underneath. They teach this face to look sultry or sexy or animated. And they call it beautiful.

True beauty is never a function of fashion or makeup. It emanates from within—from the quiet loveliness of a gentle spirit. When you sit quietly in my presence in a posture of prayer, I look at you and see the kind of beauty I appreciate.

Your Creator,
>God

== == ==   == == == == == == == == ==

WATCH WHAT YOU WATCH

I will set before my eyes no vile thing. The deeds
of faithless men I hate; they will not cling to me.

Psalm **101:3**

Dear Daughter,

>Have you ever taken a stroll through a pigpen? If so, you'll never
forget it. The odor of the animals clings to you long after you've
walked away. The same thing is true of vivid sexual descriptions in
books and unsavory scenes in movies or on television. You may think
you can simply close the book or flip off the television set and block
out the whole experience, but you can't. Those scenes and
descriptions actually cling to your spirit like barnyard slop clings to
your shoes.

You are, by nature, a spiritually sensitive being. That's the way I
created you. But I made you that way so you could absorb my
goodness, not so you could absorb the world's filth. Be careful of
what you watch, my child.

The Holy One,
>God

== == ==   == == == == == == == == ==

THE ULTIMATE GENTLEMAN

Come near to God and he will come near to you.

	James	4:8	

My Child,

>Have you heard the saying, "God is a gentleman"? It's true. Though I want a relationship with you more than anything, I'm too much of a gentleman to break down the door of your heart and rush in uninvited. But as soon as you choose to draw near to me, I'll draw near to you. As soon as you ask me to come in, I will.

And once I come into your heart, there is so much we can share. I'll help you step into your destiny. I'll help you walk in my ways. I'll clean your heart from any trace of old sinfulness, and I'll furnish the rooms of your life with righteousness. In childlike simplicity, open yourself to my love, my daughter, and I will meet you at your point of surrender.

The Ultimate Gentleman,
>God

== == ==   == == == == == == == == ==

IT'S TIME TO LOOK FORWARD

**Forget the former things; do not dwell on the past.
See, I am doing a new thing! Now it springs up;
do you not perceive it? I am making a way
in the desert and streams in the wasteland.**

| | | | | | Isaiah | 43:18-19 | | | | | |

My Child,

>Sometimes in the bleakness of winter, it's hard to believe that spring will come again. But hidden within every leafless limb and every closed and buried bulb is the beauty and life and color of springtime just waiting to happen.

Your heart may feel like a winter landscape just now, but believe me, new life is at hand. Take care of old "heart business." Confess your wrongs and let go of bitterness. Now it's time to move forward. Look! I'm doing a new thing. My plans for you are unfurling like the spring green of new leaves bursting with life.

The Lord of Springtime,
>God

== == ==   == == == == == == == == ==

D IS MY CHILD

from papyrus reeds,
put the baby in it, and
along the river's edge.

| | Exodus | 2:3 TLB | | |

My Daughter,

>Your child is only on loan to you for a season. I want you to love her as she is, but pray for her as she can be. Ask me, and I will show you her place in my kingdom. I will use your prayer to propel her toward my plans for her life.

Just as Moses' mother set her child afloat, you will eventually have to set your child out into the currents of life, trusting that I will bring her to the proper shore. Just as Mary had to face the fact about her Son in the temple, you must face the same fact: the time will come when your child must also be about my business. I have great plans for your child, just as I do for you. Trust me enough to let her go.

Your Father and Hers,
>God

== == == == == == == == == == ==

STAND STRONG!

Stand firm. Let nothing move you. Always give yourselves fully to the work of the Lord, because you know that your labor in the Lord is not in vain.

1 Corinthians 15:58

Dear Daughter,

>Have you ever tried to stand up in the surf when the tide's coming in? The waves can knock you off your feet. Life's rude surprises and changes are a lot like those waves. They can knock you flat spiritually unless you're grounded in me.

But continue in prayer throughout the changes, and I'll help you find your footing. Seek me, and I'll show you your place in the kingdom. Submit to my will, and I will stabilize you and keep you standing strong in the midst of life's swirling waves.

Your Prayer Partner,
>God

== == ==   == == == == == == == == ==

SURF'S UP!

What good is it, my brothers, if a man claims to have faith but has no deeds? Can such faith save him?

| James | 2:14 |

My Child,

>Suppose someone gives you a top-of-the-line surfboard and a manual on surfing. On day one, you read all about the board itself and how it's made. On day two, you read about the techniques of surfing. On day three, you read about safety in surfing and the history of surfing in the United States. For months you study the manual. You spend hours at the beach watching others on their surfboards. But if you never put your board in the water and feel the thrill of riding a wave, what's the point? You might as well not have it.

The same is true of your faith. You can read and believe everything about me, but if you never put your faith into action, what good is it to either of us? So how about it? Surf's up!

The Lord of Faith *and* Deeds,
>God

== == ==   == == == == == == == == ==

COME AND LET ME HEAL YOU

> Heavens and earth, be happy. Mountains, shout
> with joy, because the Lord comforts his people
> and will have pity on those who suffer.

Isaiah   49:13 NCV

Dear Child of Mine,

>I look back on your childhood and see all the times you were hurt,
intentionally or unintentionally. I hear the wounding words and see the
shaming deeds, and I know the scars you carry because of them.
Sometimes the very people you looked to for love were the ones who
hurt you most. Sometimes they were members of your own family!

But though you may have been wounded, I will never wound you.
Though you may have been let down, I will never let you down. I
speak words of hope and healing, comfort and kindness. You are
constantly on my mind. I have a great future planned for you, my
child. Come now and let me heal you.

The One Who Comforts,
>God

== == ==   == == == == == == == == ==

YOU ARE YOU. YOU ARE MINE!

The Lord spoke his word to me, saying, "Before I made you in your mother's womb, I chose you. Before you were born, I set you apart."

Jeremiah	1:4-5 NCV

My Daughter,

>When you were a child, wasn't it great to be chosen first when teams were being picked for a game? I want you to know you were chosen to be on my team from the very first. You're here for a reason. You're part of my plan.

Whenever you're tempted to feel insignificant, I want you to remind yourself how valuable you are to me. Before you were even born, I knew exactly who you would be. While you were still in the womb, I was putting you together according to my design. I didn't make any mistakes when I made you. I am filled with pride over you. Be at peace with yourself. You are chosen. You are you. You are mine!

Your Designer,
>God

== == ==   == == == == == == == == ==

NO DOUBT!

Anyone who doubts is like a wave in the sea, blown up and down by the wind. Such doubters are thinking two different things at the same time, and they cannot decide about anything they do. They should not think they will receive anything from the Lord.

James 1:6-8 NCV

My Daughter,

>Did you know that even the smallest doubt can split the sails of your faith and pull you out of the race? Everyone has doubts at times. That's why it's important to know how to handle them.

First of all, don't pretend. Tell it like it is. Next, bring each small doubt into the light, and ask me for more faith. Pray like the man who said, "I do believe! Help me to believe more!" That's a prayer I love to answer. There is no need to be tentative or shaky. I know your heart, and I can put your doubts to rest. In fact, I'll supply as much faith as you need whenever you need it. That's a promise.

The Faith Supplier,
>God

== == ==   == == == == == == == == ==

FIND ME FAITHFUL

**Just as I was with Moses, so I will be with you.
I will not leave you or forget you.**

| | Joshua | 1:5 NCV | |

My Child,

>After Moses died, I called Joshua to take his place. Can you imagine how intimidating that must have been for Joshua? The people saw Moses as a spiritual giant. Joshua could have responded, "Who, me? You've got to be kidding!" But he didn't. He didn't look to his fears or his doubts. He didn't look to other people. Instead he looked to me, and I helped him step into Moses' big shoes. He looked to me and found me faithful every step of the way into the Promised Land.

What I told Joshua, I'm telling you, my child. Just as I was with Moses, I will be with you. I don't play favorites. I'm here to guide you into your destiny. Listen and you'll hear my call on your life.

The Faithful One,
>God

== == ==   == == == == == == == == ==

LISTEN WITH YOUR LIFE

Scripture is given by God and is useful for teaching, for showing people what is wrong in their lives, for correcting faults, and for teaching how to live right.

| 2 Timothy | 3:16 NCV |

My Daughter,

>My Word is more than paper and ink, more than words and sentences. My Word is my nature, my wisdom, my guidance, my love distilled into letter form. It's health and life, truth and healing. It's the essence of who I am!

Keep my Word before your eyes. Give it permission to roam the rooms of your heart—cleaning, straightening, rearranging, closing doors on some things, opening windows on others. My Word can be for your heart a companion, a hearth, and a housekeeper, a gardener to weed your thoughts, and a guard against intruders. And so, as you open my Word today, read with your eyes, but listen with your life.

The One Who Speaks to You,
>God

== == ==   == == == == == == == == ==

I WILL EQUIP YOU

Brothers, think of what you were when you were called. Not many of you were wise by human standards. . . . But God chose the foolish things of the world to shame the wise; God chose the weak things of the world to shame the strong.

1 Corinthians   1:26-27

My Child,

>Do you really think I chose you because you were a mental genius or a spiritual giant? No. It was because you were willing to trust and follow me—willing to be used. Don't worry about what work I've got for you. I would never be so foolish as to send you out without first equipping you.

Look at how many times I've chosen a person who seemed inadequate. David seemed too small to slay a giant. Mary seemed too young to be the mother of a Savior. Moses seemed too old to deliver a nation. But I equipped them, and they got the job done. So remember, however great your assignment, my power to achieve it is greater.

The One Who Equips You,
>God

== == ==　　== == == == == == == == ==

OFFER YOUR LIFE

I urge you, brothers, in view of God's mercy, to offer your bodies as living sacrifices, holy and pleasing to God—this is your spiritual act of worship.

Romans | **12:1**

My Daughter,

>What is worship? Is it singing, praying, reading from the Bible? Is it sharing individual testimonies? All of those things can be part of a worship service. But worship itself is the specific offering of your life to me. It is lifting yourself up—body, mind, and spirit—and saying, "Take me, Father. I am yours." I want you to be more than a temple built for me; I also want you to be a temple dedicated to me so I can live in you.

That's why worshiping me is more than hoping you're mine. It is making a definite commitment to belong to me. It's gathering everything about yourself—your hopes, your dreams, your talents, even your disappointments and failures—and presenting them to me. I want all of you.

The One Who Loves Your Worship,
>God

== == ==   == == == == == == == == ==

ATTENTION TO DETAIL

Are not two sparrows sold for a penny? Yet not one of them will fall to the ground apart from the will of your Father. And even the very hairs of your head are all numbered. So don't be afraid; you are worth more than many sparrows.

Matthew | 10:29-31

Dearest Child,

>You live in a culture of assembly lines cranking out mass-manufactured products. It is a rarity to find a unique product that has been distinctively crafted with care. When you find yourself longing to look at careful crafting and exquisite workmanship, consider my world. Look at my flowers, birds, and butterflies. I paid attention to every detail, and no two are exactly alike.

And you, my child, are the pride of my creation—beautiful, intelligent, amazing! I paid enormous attention to detail in creating you. So how can you ever be tempted to think I'm not interested in every little problem or decision you face, every small celebration or success in your life? I care about all the details of my intricate creation.

The Master Craftsman,
>God

== == ==   == == == == == == == == ==

WALK MY TALK

The man who looks intently into the perfect law that gives freedom, and continues to do this, not forgetting what he has heard, but doing it—he will be blessed in what he does.

| James | 1:25 |

Child of Mine,

>Many Christians "talk a good game," but their actions don't follow their talk. They can quote chapter and verse of the Bible on forgiveness, for instance, but if you could see into their hearts, you would find unforgiveness hiding there.

My child, studying the Word and following it are both important to me. How will you know me if you don't read my words? And how will you honor me if you don't follow them? My words are words of freedom, but they can't free you from anything unless you take them off the page and put them into practice. Beginning today, my child, I want you to take my Word personally and practice it daily. Learn the talk, and then walk the walk.

The One Who Speaks,
>God

== == ==   == == == == == == == == ==

DON'T BE A LOOSE CANNON

Speaking the truth in love, we will in all things grow up into him who is the Head, that is, Christ.

| Ephesians | 4:15 |

My Daughter,

>Truth can be like a cannonball. When it is fired at someone's heart with no regard for that person's feelings, it can be deadly. Have you ever known someone who is a "loose cannon"? When she opens her mouth, she takes aim at anyone and everyone and leaves wounded people in the wake of her words. She even acts as though her honesty were a virtue.

But honesty without love is far from virtuous. I don't talk to you that way, and I don't want you talking that way to anyone else. When I speak a word of truth to you—even a hard word—it will always come to you dressed in a coat of encouragement. Let me help you speak the truth in love to the people in your life.

The Truth and the Love,
>God

== == ==   == == == == == == == == ==

KEEP ON KEEPING ON

**When they could not find a way to do this because
of the crowd, they went up on the roof and lowered him
on his mat through the tiles into the middle of the crowd,
right in front of Jesus. When Jesus saw their faith,
he said, "Friend, your sins are forgiven."**

Luke 5:19-20

Dear Child of Mine,

>Pray with purpose. Seek my answers with determination. Pursue me like the men who so desperately desired the healing of their paralyzed friend that they refused to be stopped. When they couldn't get close to Jesus because of the crowd, they lowered their friend through the roof on his mattress into my Son's presence!

Don't let anything keep you from coming into my presence. Pray fervently. Bring your needs to me and lay them at my feet. Forgiveness and healing will follow. Come to me now.

Your Answer,
>God

== == ==   == == == == == == == == ==

THERE IS A PURPOSE

**All who claim me as their God will come,
for I have made them for my glory;
I created them. Bring them back to me.**

Isaiah | **43:7-8 TLB**

My Precious Child,

>So many people this very day will be waking up, dressing for work, eating breakfast, and stepping into the drudgery of their lives without any sense of why they exist. The purpose of every life is simple and beautiful. It is to give me glory. It is to allow me to shine all the light and beauty and power of who I am through the unique personality of who they are until the whole world is filled with my glory.

So spread the word: "God Emmanuel is with us! He has made us for this purpose—to know him, to contain his Spirit, to celebrate his love!" This is the good news that will bring my children home.

Your Loving Father,
>God

== == ==   == == == == == == == == ==

CLING TO MY PROMISES

I will pour water on the thirsty land, and streams on the dry ground; I will pour out my Spirit on your offspring, and my blessing on your descendants. They will spring up like grass in a meadow, like poplar trees by flowing streams.

Isaiah   44:3-4

My Daughter,

>I know the longing of every Christian mother's heart is that her children would come to know me. That longing is also mine. I wait for the day when each one will run into my arms, because your children are my children too.

But they cannot come to me clinging to the coattails of your faith. Each one must find his or her own faith and make his or her own choice. I have promised to bring your children home and pour out my Spirit on them. But it's not up to you to make those promises come true. You can't nag your children into my arms. Instead, cling to my promises, praying in faith, and watch them turn toward home.

The Father of Your Children,
>God

== == ==   == == == == == == == == ==

THE JOY OF THE SPIRIT WALK

The mystery in a nutshell is just this: Christ is in you, therefore you can look forward to sharing in God's glory. It's that simple.

| Colossians | 1:27 The Message |

My Daughter,

>When you belong to me, I take up residence in your heart. When your heart is my home, I live out my life in the center of your daily decisions and affections and activities. As long as you stay in relationship with me, as long as you yield to my Spirit in you, your thoughts will be the ones I think, your choices will be the ones I make, and your activities will be the ones I enjoy.

You don't need to keep taking your spiritual temperature every ten minutes, saying, "How am I doing? Am I being righteous enough?" You'll know the freedom of the God-inhabited life, the joy of the Spirit-walk. And every day you'll understand a little more clearly what Jesus meant when he said, "I do only what I see my Father doing." That's what I call glory.

The Life in You,
>God

== == ==   == == == == == == == == ==

WHAT DO YOU WORSHIP?

**Who but a fool would make his own god—
an idol that can help him not one whit!**

Isaiah 44:10 TLB

Dear Child,

>When you read accounts of ancient people groups bowing down to stone idols, you probably think how backward and unenlightened they were. Actually there are probably people in your neighborhood whose hearts are "bowing down" to their houses, which are nothing but stacks of stones, or to their automobiles, which are nothing but hunks of metal, or to their wardrobes, which are nothing but cuts of cloth. They may not even know that they've got a worship situation going on, but I know. When a person spends the largest part of her thought and energy and care on something other than me, that thing is her god.

Do some soul-searching. Am I really the one you worship? Make me—

Your One and Only,
>God

== == ==   == == == == == == == == ==

HIS VICTORY WAS YOURS

So spacious is he, so roomy, that everything of God
finds its proper place in him . . . all the broken and
dislocated pieces of the universe . . . get properly fixed
and fit together in vibrant harmonies, all because of
his death, his blood that poured down from the Cross.

Colossians **1:20 THE MESSAGE**

My Child,

>People looked at Jesus when he walked the Galilean countryside
and saw nothing spectacular—a common working man with rough
hands, dressed in a homespun robe. Little did they know that this one
who talked and laughed and ate his meals with them contained the
destiny of the universe. In him was the power to heal my children and
reconcile my lost world to me.

The blood he spilled as he hung bruised and battered on the cross
seemed a cruel tragedy. His death and his burial seemed an awful
waste. But when the stone rolled away and he burst through the doors
of death into my eternity, his story was total victory. Your victory!

His Father and Yours,
>God

== == ==   == == == == == == == == ==

TIPPED OVER BY MY PRESENCE

Arise, my people! Let your light shine for all the nations to see! For the glory of the Lord is streaming from you.

Isaiah 60:1 TLB

My Daughter,

>Christians love to talk about my glory, yet very few of them can come up with a definition for it. It's more than the usual synonyms like magnificence, splendor, wonder, grandeur, and brilliance. It's an awesome experience of being filled with and tipped over by my presence. When you are in a vibrant, ongoing relationship with me, my glory is all over you. It streams out of you to others around you.

Today I am encouraging you, my child, to recommit yourself to our relationship. Come into my presence and let me set your heart ablaze with the fire of my glory so that you can go out and light up the world.

Your Glorious Father,
>God

== == ==   == == == == == == == == ==

SOMEONE STEPPED BETWEEN YOU AND JUSTICE

At one time you all had your backs turned to God, . . . giving him trouble every chance you got. But now, by giving himself completely at the Cross, actually dying for you, Christ brought you over to God's side and put your lives together, whole and holy in his presence.

Colossians | 1:21 THE MESSAGE

My Daughter,

>Can you look back on a time when your heart was far from me—a time when rebellion was a way of life—when loving me and following me were the last things on your mind? Every law-breaking choice you made then could have had eternal consequences.

But before you could even keep your appointment in the courtroom, before the judge could even hear your case, someone stepped between you and the justice you deserved. When Jesus died, he took the consequences for your lawlessness on himself. He said, "I'll take the rap." When He rose again, he made a way for you, an outlaw, to step out of that lifestyle and come home to me.

The One Who Welcomes You,
>God

== == ==   == == == == == == == == ==

A CURE FOR STRESS

**Great peace have they who love your law,
and nothing can make them stumble.**

| Psalm | 119:165 |

My Child,

>One of the most coveted commodities in modern life is inner peace.
Notice the next time you're in the checkout line at the supermarket
how many magazine covers feature articles on how to reduce stress.
Stress-free lives are in the minority among people in your culture.
Where do you go for inner peace? Some people rely on overeating,
overdrinking, or prescription drugs. Some find that a shopping spree
calms the anxiety inside—but not for long.

Here is my prescription for stress-free living (and you can't fill it at
your druggist's counter). Come to me, and I will give you rest. Read
my Word. Know my Son. Receive my Spirit. Then feel the peace
that follows.

The One Who Calms Your Storms,
>God

== == ==   == == == == == == == == ==

DO WHAT NEEDS TO BE DONE

**Listen now! The Lord isn't too weak to save you.
And he isn't getting deaf! He can hear you when you call!
But the trouble is that your sins have cut you off from God.**

Isaiah 59:1–2 TLB

Dear Child,

>Don't think I haven't heard you calling me. Don't think I've put you on hold. I want to help you. But there's something standing between us. Be quiet in my presence and listen to what my Spirit in you is trying to say. Take pen and paper with you. Write down what you hear in your heart. Is there someone whose forgiveness you need to seek? Is there someone who has wronged you whom you have not forgiven? Is there something that I've told you to do that you still haven't done? Some behavior I've asked you to change? Some attitude I've asked you to adjust?

These things (whatever they are) stand between you and me. Please, my child, don't let anything keep us apart. Take care of business today.

Your Father,
>God

== == ==   == == == == == == == == ==

CHUCK THE RELIGION

**Don't put up with anyone pressuring you in
details of diet, worship services, or holy days.
All those things were mere shadows cast before
what was to come; the substance is Christ.**

Colossians 2:16 The Message

My Child,

>Don't listen to people who want to tell you how to "do" religion. Don't
get tangled up in all the rules that say things like, "Dress this way but
not that way," or "Worship this way but not that way." Some people
love religion. They can feel comfortable and safe and righteous if they
get everything "right."

Religion is your attempt to reach me through your efforts. But
Christianity is not about religion. It's about you having a personal
relationship with me. And that relationship is based on my hand
reaching down to touch you with my grace. Chuck the religion, and
let's get on with the relationship.

Your Father,
>God

== == ==   == == == == == == == == ==

SO MANY DISGUISES

Do not forget to entertain strangers, for by so doing some people have entertained angels without knowing it.

| Hebrews | 13:2 |

My Daughter,

>Have you ever had a surprise visit from a neighbor—a child or an adult—who caught you at your busiest time of day? What were your unspoken thoughts at the time? *Oh, great! Another interruption. Just exactly what I don't need.*

I want to tell you something about surprise guests and unexpected interruptions. Often they are emissaries from me—messengers who break into your busyness to check your heart attitude. So don't get so caught up in your own agenda that you shut out my messengers. If you opened your door and saw an angel on your doorstep, wouldn't you let him in? Who knows, maybe that dirty child or that cranky old woman from down the street is really my angel in disguise. Welcome them.

The Lord of Many Disguises,
>God

== == ==   == == == == == == == == ==

HOLD THAT PICTURE

Lift up your eyes and see! For your sons and daughters are coming home to you from distant lands. Your eyes will shine with joy, your hearts will thrill.

Isaiah 60:4-5 TLB

My Daughter,

I want to set a picture in your heart—a picture that will inspire you to pray for your children. Look with the eyes of your heart and see your own son or daughter coming home to me. Picture your own prodigal child, moving joyfully, hopefully toward me and my kingdom.

On that day, you'll realize how little your everyday worries have mattered. On that day, you'll set them all aside and rush down the road with me to greet your beloved child, the one you've waited for. There will be a ring for his finger, a robe for his shoulders, and a celebration with the family of faith. Hold that picture and pray toward that reality.

Your Faithful Father,
>God

== == ==   == == == == == == == == ==

YOU FEED 'EM, FELLAS!

He replied, "You give them something to eat."
They answered, "We have only five loaves of bread and
two fish—unless we go and buy food for all this crowd."

| Luke | 9:13 |

Dear Child,

>My Son must have been smiling inside when he asked his disciples
to feed the crowd. He knew they would feel a twinge of momentary
panic. But that's how he got their attention. "You feed 'em, fellas!" he
said. What could they do but look to Jesus? That's when He asked
them to bring their meager resources to him, and he worked a miracle.

What amazement they must have felt as they looked out at the giant
picnic they had just hosted! And when it was over, there were twelve
baskets of leftovers. This is a picture of my grace. Bring what you
have to Jesus (even if it's not much), and he will use your resources
to bless others in ways you never dreamed of.

The Lord of Grace and Power,
>God

== == ==   == == == == == == == == ==

LET'S COOPERATE

**God did not call us to be impure,
but to live a holy life.**

| | | | | 1 Thessalonians | 4:7 | | | | | |

My Child,

>How does the word "holiness" hit you? Does it seem like an
outdated and old-fashioned concept? Does it sound like a destination
too removed from everyday reality for you to reach?

I want you to be holy, but I'm not asking you to get there in your own
power. In fact, that's not even possible. Your holiness is going to
involve cooperation between your humanity and my deity. It will
involve my filling your spiritual tank with the grace of my Son and the
power of my Spirit. But you'll still have to turn the key, put your life in
gear, and stay on the narrow road.

Your Map and Navigator,
>God

== == ==   == == == == == == == == ==

LIVING ON TWO LEVELS

If you're serious about living this new resurrection life . . . act like it. Pursue the things over which Christ presides. Don't shuffle along, eyes to the ground, absorbed with the things right in front of you. Look up, and be alert to what is going on around Christ— that's where the action is. See things from his perspective.

Colossians | 3:1-2 The Message

My Daughter,

>It's easy to let your life get sucked into the humdrum, daily plane of existence, pounding out the repetitive drumbeat of the here and now. But there is so much more to life than being up on your laundry, your housework, your job responsibilities. You can take care of these things without letting them totally absorb you.

You were created to live on another, more spiritual plane as well. There is wonder and beauty and self-discovery waiting on this spiritual plane. You don't have to move to a foreign country or buy a new wardrobe to experience it. Jesus is holding out his adventure in the midst of your daily life. Open your eyes and your heart to what he has for you on this spiritual plane.

His Father and Yours,
>God

== == ==   == == == == == == == == ==

I'LL KEEP YOU YOUNG

[The everlasting God] gives power to the tired and
worn out, and strength to the weak. . . . They that wait
upon the Lord shall renew their strength. They shall
mount up with wings like eagles; they shall run
and not be weary; they shall walk and not faint.

Isaiah   40:29,31 TLB

My Precious One,

>The world you live in is obsessed with staying young. Every day you
see people spending enormous amounts of time, energy, and money
on any scheme that promises to keep them youthful. Some have
mastered the art of looking young on the outside, but on the inside
their spirits have lost their youthfulness.

Trying to maintain a youthful appearance is not a sin, but stressing
the physical over the spiritual is a turn down the wrong road. I am the
God who lives forever. If you seek me, I will keep your spirit alive and
kicking, even when your body begins to age. Let me keep you young.

The Everlasting One,
>God

LESSONS OF PEACE

He replied, "You of little faith, why are you so afraid?"

Matthew 8:26

My Daughter,

>I teach you lessons of peace in different ways, depending on what you need. Sometimes when you have already let panic set in, I may step in and calm the storm of fear just as I did for the disciples. But at other times I use the storm itself to grow your faith. I allow the winds to rage and the rain to fall, and as you call out to me, I calm your heart rather than calming the storm. I teach you not to trust in the weather or the boat or the outward appearance of things but in my Son, who is your peace.

Keep your eyes on me in the midst of whatever tries to ruffle the waters of your life today, whether it is major trouble or a very small problem. I can handle both.

The Lord of Peace,
>God

== == ==   == == == == == == == == ==

MAKE THIS SAME CHOICE

Shadrach, Meshach, and Abednego replied, "O Nebuchadnezzar, we are not worried about what will happen to us. If we are thrown into the flaming furnace, our God is able to deliver us. . . . But if he doesn't, please understand, sir, that even then we will never under any circumstance serve your gods or worship the golden statue.

Daniel 3:16–18 TLB

My Daughter,

>The story of Shadrach and his two friends has a contemporary ring to it. At this very moment many people in different parts of the world are being persecuted for their faith in me. Even in your country you may have experienced prejudice against your beliefs. You may have felt pressure to deny them.

I encourage you to look at the attitudes of these three young men. They were totally sold out to me. They firmly believed that I could deliver them from the fire, but they had made their choice to stand firm regardless—to stay true whether I chose to deliver them or not. Make this same choice in your own life, and you will know my peace in the midst of turmoil.

The One Who Is Able,
>God

== == ==   == == == == == == == == ==

A NEW WARDROBE

Dress in the wardrobe God picked out for you: compassion, kindness, humility, quiet strength, discipline. Be even-tempered, content with second place. . . . Forgive as quickly as the Master forgave you. And regardless of what else you put on, wear love. It's your basic, all-purpose garment.

Colossians 3:12-13 THE MESSAGE

My Daughter,

>Suppose I gave you an unlimited budget and sent you out to shop for the perfect wardrobe. Wouldn't you love that assignment? Well, you don't have to shop for the perfect spiritual wardrobe. I've already done that.

The spiritual garments I've chosen will suit you perfectly, because you were made to wear them. Dress your heart in the compassion of Jesus and in his kindness. Dress your spirit in his humility and quiet strength. Dress your will in his discipline and your mind in his contentment. But the most beautiful garment in your spiritual wardrobe will be worn over them all. It's an all-weather coat of love that covers a multitude of failures.

Your Wardrobe Consultant,
>God

== == ==   == == == == == == == == ==

THEY ARE ALL AROUND YOU

The Spirit of the Sovereign Lord is on me, because the Lord has anointed me to preach good news to the poor. He has sent me to bind up the brokenhearted, to proclaim freedom for the captives and release from darkness for the prisoners.

| | | Isaiah | | 61:1 | | | |

My Daughter,

>I have equipped you to bring good news to a needy world—to bandage broken hearts and unlock prison doors. The needy ones are all around you. Your coworker at the next desk may desperately need a friend. Invite her to have coffee with you. The woman who styles your hair may be going through a heartbreaking divorce. Check on her between appointments. Invite her to lunch or to church. The widow in the next block may be recovering from surgery and may be unable to drive. Take her grocery shopping or offer to do her shopping. In simple ways, you can begin to reach out and love my world for me right where you are.

The Lord Who Anoints You,
>God

== == ==   == == == == == == == == ==

THE WISE HEART LISTENS

**The wise in heart accept commands,
but a chattering fool comes to ruin.**

| Proverbs | 10:8 |

Dear Child of Mine,

>Expressing your own opinion on every subject is easy. Putting in your two cents' worth can be fun. But being quiet and listening is difficult. Have you ever found yourself in a conversation with someone else, just waiting for that person to finish so you can have your say?

I don't want you to be that way with me. When we spend time together I love to hear your prayers, but I also have things I want to say to you. I want to encourage you, to guide you, to map out instructions for your life. But how can you hear me if you are so busy expressing your own ideas that you never sit still and listen to mine? I encourage you to have a wise and listening heart.

The One Who Speaks,
>God

== == ==   == == == == == == == == ==

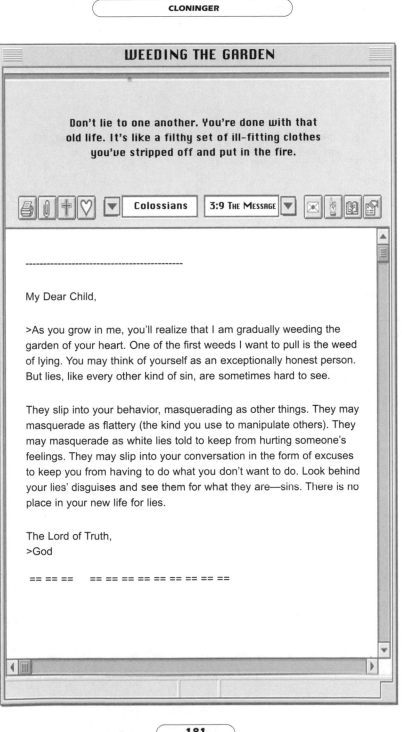

WEEDING THE GARDEN

Don't lie to one another. You're done with that
old life. It's like a filthy set of ill-fitting clothes
you've stripped off and put in the fire.

| Colossians | 3:9 The Message |

My Dear Child,

>As you grow in me, you'll realize that I am gradually weeding the
garden of your heart. One of the first weeds I want to pull is the weed
of lying. You may think of yourself as an exceptionally honest person.
But lies, like every other kind of sin, are sometimes hard to see.

They slip into your behavior, masquerading as other things. They may
masquerade as flattery (the kind you use to manipulate others). They
may masquerade as white lies told to keep from hurting someone's
feelings. They may slip into your conversation in the form of excuses
to keep you from having to do what you don't want to do. Look behind
your lies' disguises and see them for what they are—sins. There is no
place in your new life for lies.

The Lord of Truth,
>God

== == ==   == == == == == == == == ==

YOU WERE MADE FOR THIS

Stand up and praise the LORD your God, who is from everlasting to everlasting. Blessed be your glorious name, and may it be exalted above all blessing and praise.

Nehemiah | 9:5

My Daughter,

>How long has it been since you've stood up and praised me with total abandon? I see far more excitement and enthusiasm among people of the world cheering for football games or political rallies or stock market returns than I do from many of my children worshiping me. Look at those sports fans, for instance. They go wild, clapping and cheering. There's no doubt about how they feel.

In a world where many speak my name as a swearword, isn't it about time you stood up and proclaimed it with enthusiasm and joy? Whenever or wherever you worship me, put your whole heart into it. You were created to worship this way.

The One Who's Worthy,
>God

== == ==   == == == == == == == == ==

LET MY LOVE HEAL YOU

Everything we know about God's Word is summed up in a single sentence: Love others as you love yourself.

Galatians | 5:14 THE MESSAGE

My Daughter,

>It's a good thing to love others as you love yourself. But what if you don't love yourself very much? What if you're always critical of yourself, focusing only on your flaws and never on your good points? In that case, it wouldn't be a very good thing to pass that kind of critical, conditional love on to others.

So here's my suggestion: Let my love heal your vision of who you are. Let me show you what I see in you—all of your strengths and your gifts and your tremendous potential. And then, as you begin to love yourself with a healthy self-love, you'll begin to be ready to love others as I have called you to.

The Perfect Love,
>God

== == ==   == == == == == == == == ==

LET YOUR ROOTS GO DEEP

To all who mourn . . . he will give: beauty for ashes; joy instead of mourning; praise instead of heaviness. For God has planted them like strong and graceful oaks for his own glory.

Isaiah   **61:3** TLB

My Daughter,

>Animals have learned that in dry seasons there is no moisture near the surface of the soil, so they dig below the surface to find water that will quench their thirst. Thirsty trees also send their roots down deep to reach underground pockets of water.

During your seasons of sorrow, my child, let your roots go down deep into my love for you. Let my living water satisfy your thirsty spirit. Though now you may see only the charred ashes of your life, trust me. I am in the process of renewing you. You can trade those ashes for beauty, trade your mourning for my joy, and trade your troubled spirit for my song of praise. Dig down deep, and your healing will spring forth.

Your Healer,
>God

== == ==   == == == == == == == == ==

MY POWER IS JUST A PRAYER AWAY

**With your help I can advance against
a troop; with my God I can scale a wall.**

| Psalm | 18:29 |

My Child,

>Look at the heroes of the Bible. David, Esther, Joshua, Moses, Mary—
these were not physical or spiritual giants. They were just simple men
and women who were willing to pray with faith and act with courage.
They were just ordinary people who trusted an extraordinary God,
and through them great things were done.

What about you? What am I asking you to do for me today? Whether
it's feeding the hungry people of the world or rocking one fussy baby,
I'll give you the strength you need to do it. There is no greater joy for
me than pouring my power into your weakness and watching great
things happen.

Your Power,
>God

== == ==   == == == == == == == == ==

IT'S A NEW DAY

[Jesus] took [the dead girl] by the hand and said, "My child, get up!" Her spirit returned, and at once she stood up.

Luke 8:54-55

My Daughter,

>Sometimes it's not the huge, heroic challenges that are the hardest to face but the small, ordinary things of life—turning off the alarm clock, putting your feet on the floor, making the coffee, changing the baby, driving the carpool.

Today, if you've got the feeling you're on an endless conveyer belt of activities, I want to wake you up to my presence in the midst of your life. In all of these potentially boring situations, Jesus is saying, "Get up, my child! It's a new day!" If his love was powerful enough to raise a dead girl, it is certainly powerful enough to help you get through this day with hope and humor.

The Father of the Ordinary,
>God

== == ==   == == == == == == == == ==

WHY WORRY?

So don't worry at all about having enough food and clothing.
Why be like the heathen? For they take pride in all these things
and are deeply concerned about them. But your heavenly
Father already knows perfectly well that you need them, and
he will give them to you if you give him first place in your life.

Matthew **6:31–33** TLB

My Child,

>Why is trust so hard for you? Why do you worry about menus
and calories and what the scale will say when you step on it? Why
do you fret about styles and fashions and pulling together just the
right wardrobe?

Life is so much more than food; your body is so much more than the
clothes you put on it. Look at the birds. They have never made a
grocery list or counted a calorie, yet they get fed. Look at a field of
flowers. Do you think they worry about what's in style or what color
goes with what? If I take care of birds and flowers, can't you believe
I'll take care of you? Put me first, and I will.

The One Who Loves You,
>God

== == ==   == == == == == == == == ==

CALLING HOME

The Lord will hear me when I call to him.

| Psalm | 4:3 NKJV |

My Daughter,

>How many times do you make a business call and find yourself on hold, complete with canned music blaring in your ear? How often does call-waiting beep in on your conversation with a friend and leave you holding a silent receiver while she checks her other caller?

Don't worry about those things happening when you call on me. I will never put you on hold; I don't even have call-waiting. In fact, I'm so anxious to talk to you, I've given you your very own personal-access 800 number so you can call me toll free any time of the day or night. There's no excuse for not calling home.

Your Father,
>God

== == ==   == == == == == == == == ==

A SPIRITUAL RENAISSANCE

**They shall rebuild the ancient ruins, repairing
cities long ago destroyed, reviving them
though they have lain there many generations.**

	Isaiah	61:4 TLB	

My Child,

>In your country there are many places where the faith of your
fathers lies in disrepair. The spiritual fire that once burned bright has
grown dim.

I am calling my people to start a Christian renaissance in your
country. I am calling you to be one of those renaissance women—to
stand for truth and to pray for righteousness. I am calling you to
rebuild "the ancient ruins" by fanning the flames of faith in your own
family, church, and city. As you work beside fellow renaissance
Christians, you will see the ruins repaired and the spiritual devastation
turned into revival. Trust me for this rebirth of faith in your country.

The Rebuilder,
>God

== == ==   == == == == == == == == ==

THE TRUEST ANSWER

I have put aside all else, counting it worth less than nothing in order that I can have Christ, and become one with him.

| Philippians | 3:8-9 TLB |

My Child,

>Everything in your life (family, career, ministry) is a gift from me. Since you pour your time and your heart into these things, you naturally get a lot out of them. But I don't want you to believe that these things define you. No matter how important they seem, they are merely things that you do, not who you are.

I want to be the passion that defines your life. I want you to know who you are in me—an incredibly loved child of God. You are always accepted, always protected, always secure in me. So when someone asks, "What do you do?" instead of saying, "I'm a mother," or "I'm a computer analyst," say instead, "I am God's child." That's the truest answer.

The Source of Your Identity,
>God

== == ==   == == == == == == == == ==

PERFECT PLANS

"I know what I am planning for you," says the Lord.
"I have good plans for you, not plans to hurt you.
I will give you hope and a good future."

| 🖨 📎 ✝ ♡ ▼ | Jeremiah | 29:11 NCV | ▼ ✉ ✍ 📖 🗒 |

My Daughter,

>When builders are in the middle of a project, it looks like a war zone.
Materials are strewn about, foundation dirt is all over the place, and
nothing looks like it makes any sense. But the construction foreman,
who has the plan, is able to see the end result, even in the middle of
the project.

Today, your future may look bleak or shadowy. But if you could see
what great plans I have for you, you would be rejoicing. Even if it
seems like bits and pieces of your life are strewn about in no particular
order, I can see my plans being fulfilled in you. Don't go worrying
about every little detail of what's to come. Just hang in there. I am
building you to my perfect specifications.

Your Architect,
>God

== == ==   == == == == == == == == ==

YOU WEAR ME WELL

**Let me tell you how happy God has made me!
For he has clothed me with garments of salvation
and draped about me the robe of righteousness.**

| Isaiah | 61:10 TLB |

My Daughter,

>When you spend time with me, when you listen for my voice and hear the words I whisper to your heart, you won't be able to keep the joy inside yourself. It will bubble out of you like the water of a brook. It will flow out of you like the music of a song. You won't have thoughts like, *I know I should be talking more about my faith.* In the most natural, unpreachy way, the reality of your faith is going to show up on your face and in your conversation.

Suppose you were wearing a gorgeous, perfectly fitting dress of an exquisite fabric. Wouldn't people notice? The same will be true of the garments of salvation and the robe of righteousness I have given you to wear. You look great in my love.

Your Father,
>God

== == ==   == == == == == == == == ==

I'M NOT HIDING

You will search for me. And when you search for me with all your heart, you will find me!

Jeremiah 29:13 NCV

Dearest Child,

>I'm not playing spiritual hide-and-seek with you. Just the opposite! I'm right here, and when you're ready to find me, you will. You'll find me when you seek me with all your heart—when you're through playing intellectual games, when you stop trying to create me in your image, when you stop giving me ultimatums and deadlines and telling me how God should act, when it's really me you want and not some deity of your own design.

I am the God of the garden, the flood, the wilderness, and the mountaintop. I am the God of the cross, the grave, the resurrection, and the life. I am the Father of Jesus, and I am your Father too.

I Am Who I Am,
>God

== == ==   == == == == == == == == ==

SUBMERGE IT ALL

**A certain man named Ananias, with Sapphira his wife,
sold a possession, and kept back part of the price,
his wife also being privy to it, and brought a
certain part, and laid it at the apostles' feet.**

| Acts | 5:1-2 KJV |

My Child,

>During the crusades of the twelfth century, some crusaders paid
mercenary warriors to fight in their places. Because it was a war
fought for "religious" reasons, the crusaders required the mercenaries
to be baptized before going into battle. As they were being baptized,
some of the mercenaries let themselves go under water but held their
swords out because they didn't want to submit the use of their swords
to Jesus.

What is it that you are holding out of the water right now in your
Christian walk? Don't be afraid to submerge everything in me. Let me
bring those high and dry areas under my cleansing, healing waters.
Then I can use everything about you as a blessing in my world.

Your Father,
>God

== == ==   == == == == == == == == ==

DON'T CHOOSE THE WORLD

Do not love the world or the things in the world. If you love the world, the love of the Father is not in you.

| 1 John | 2:15 NCV |

My Dearest Child,

>Do you ever comparison shop to see which store is offering the best value? Today I want you to compare what the world is offering to what I'm offering. The choice is yours.

The world holds out happiness that depends on circumstances. I hold out joy. The world holds out self-serving motives and hidden agendas. I offer unconditional love. The world holds out blame and shame and condemnation. I hold out forgiveness and a new beginning. The world holds out addictions, compulsions, and momentary gratification. I fill you with peace that passes understanding. The world offers broken vows and contracts. I give you my Word, which never changes. The world offers a sad imitation of life.

I Am Life,
>God

== == ==   == == == == == == == == ==

TRUST ME WITH THE OUTCOME

**My God will supply every need of yours
according to his riches in glory in Christ Jesus.**

| | | | | ▼ | Philippians | 4:19 RSV | ▼ | | | | |

My Daughter,

>Suppose the most acclaimed pastry chef in the world gave you his
world-famous recipe for your husband's favorite cake so you could
bake it for his birthday. The chef bought all the ingredients, laid them
out in order, and explained the recipe. If you followed directions, you
wouldn't have to worry about the results.

If you are doing the best you can to follow my will, then you can leave
the results to me. I have given you my word of instruction. I've laid out
your plan to salvation and the abundant life. You don't have to sit
around and fret about what your life will look like when it comes out of
the oven. It's going to be a culinary masterpiece.

The Master Chef,
>God

== == ==   == == == == == == == == ==

JUST PRAY!

Lord, every morning you hear my voice. Every morning, I tell you what I need, and I wait for your answer.

Psalm 5:3 NCV

My Daughter,

>Prayer is not complicated. It's very simple. It's a conversation between your heart and mine. It's a place where your questions and my answers meet. It's the breath of my Holy Spirit fanning the flames of your faith. Don't worry about prayer. Don't intellectualize it. Just pray.

You will learn to pray best by praying. When you don't know where to start, start with praise. When you don't feel worthy, repent and I'll forgive. When you can't find the words, don't struggle. My Spirit knows how to express your longing better than you do. Come needy. Drink deeply. Praise freely.

The One Who Waits to Meet You,
>God

== == ==   == == == == == == == == ==

THE QUESTION ONLY YOU CAN ANSWER

Jesus asked, "But who do you say I am?"
Peter answered, "You are the Christ."

| | Mark | 8:29 NCV | |

My Child,

>Suppose you were on a game show and the host told you that your answer to the next question would change your life forever. Pretty intense moment! Jesus asked Peter a question that really did have that kind of importance. "Who do you say I am?" Jesus asked. No authority on earth could have helped Peter answer. His answer was a totally personal response. To Peter, Jesus was the Christ, and he said so.

Who is Jesus to you? Is he the Son of God as he claimed, or is he a con man or an irrelevant prophet? Your answer to this question will determine the way you live your life. The way you view who he is will mold your character and change your future. It will move you through the very gates of eternity.

The One Who Waits for Your Answer,
>God

== == ==   == == == == == == == == ==

EVEN I RESTED

**Remember to observe the Sabbath as a holy day.
Six days a week are for your daily duties and your
regular work, but the seventh day is a day of
Sabbath rest before the Lord your God.**

Exodus | 20:8-10 TLB

My Child,

>Has it ever occurred to you that even I rested on the seventh day?
Do you really think I was tired? No way. I never run out of energy. So
why did I rest? Because rest is part of the rhythm of my creation. It is
woven into the fabric of my plan.

Work can become an addiction. It constantly pushes you to do one
more thing—to achieve one more goal. Sabbath invites you to honor
me by slowing down and putting me first. It is a day set apart for my
love to refresh you. I can do more for you in one-seventh of your
week than you could ever do by pushing through and wearing
yourself out. Honor me with your Sabbath, and I'll send you back to
work bursting with fresh inspiration.

The Author of the Third Commandment,
>God

== == ==   == == == == == == == == ==

LIKE FATHER, LIKE SON

Jesus replied, "Don't you even yet know who I am,
Philip, even after all this time I have been
with you? Anyone who has seen me has seen
the Father! So why are you asking to see him?"

| John | 14:9 TLB |

My Daughter,

>How can you understand a love like mine—a love that stoops to
conquer, a love that reaches to redeem? Look at the life of my Son,
and you will see me. Look at the one who was willing to leave crowns
and thrones and angels' praises to become a baby born in a stable.
Look at the one who bowed to be baptized though he had never
sinned. Look at him who bore abuse and torture, who bled and finally
died so that you could live to laugh and love and be reconciled to me.

All you need to know of me, you will see in my Son, your Savior. Look
to Him; then turn to me.

His Father and Yours,
>God

== == ==   == == == == == == == == ==

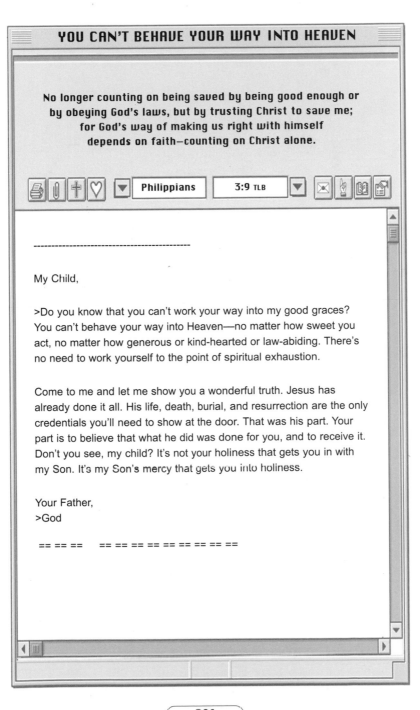

YOU CAN'T BEHAVE YOUR WAY INTO HEAVEN

No longer counting on being saved by being good enough or by obeying God's laws, but by trusting Christ to save me; for God's way of making us right with himself depends on faith—counting on Christ alone.

Philippians 3:9 TLB

My Child,

>Do you know that you can't work your way into my good graces? You can't behave your way into Heaven—no matter how sweet you act, no matter how generous or kind-hearted or law-abiding. There's no need to work yourself to the point of spiritual exhaustion.

Come to me and let me show you a wonderful truth. Jesus has already done it all. His life, death, burial, and resurrection are the only credentials you'll need to show at the door. That was his part. Your part is to believe that what he did was done for you, and to receive it. Don't you see, my child? It's not your holiness that gets you in with my Son. It's my Son's mercy that gets you into holiness.

Your Father,
>God

== == ==   == == == == == == == == ==

BE HAPPY

Those who want to do right more than anything else are happy, because God will fully satisfy them.

Matthew   5:6 NCV

My Daughter,

>When you find yourself longing for more of me—more guidance, more courage, more comfort, more company—that's the time to be happy. Why? Because you're going to get what you want. I guarantee it! When you find yourself sick of your old selfish self and your old selfish life, be glad. That's when the new life of the redeemed self begins to open like a flower!

Nothing is more compelling to me than the man or woman who has really had it with sin, who's really hungry for a fresh start. I will move Heaven and earth to give that person what he or she wants. Why? Because it's exactly what I want too. If you want more, come and be satisfied.

The Lord of New Life,
>God

== == ==   == == == == == == == == ==

BEYOND YOUR WILDEST DREAMS

Now glory be to God who by his mighty power at work within us is able to do far more than we would ever dare to ask or even dream of—infinitely beyond our highest prayers, desires, thoughts, or hopes.

| Ephesians | 3:20 TLB |

My Child,

>Sometimes I think you don't exactly realize who you're dealing with when you pray to me. You tiptoe hesitantly into my presence and say things like, "If you could possibly—" or "Could you try to figure out some sort of solution?"

Listen. Everything's possible to me, and I have unlimited solutions at my fingertips. I've got bigger, better, more amazing things for you than you could ever even dream up to ask me for. Your imagination can't begin to wrap itself around what I can do—things beyond your most fervent prayer, deeper than your deepest desire, higher than your highest hope. So stretch your faith, my daughter. Think big and ask boldly. I plan to do some of my best work in you.

The One with the Answers,
>God

== == ==   == == == == == == == == ==

A SACK OF WORRIES

Let him have all your worries and cares, for he is always thinking about you and watching everything that concerns you.

| 🖨 📎 ✝ ♡ | ▼ | 1 Peter | 5:7 TLB | ▼ | ✉ ✎ 📖 📋 |

My Dear Daughter,

>Every time you pick up a worry, it's like putting a brick in a sack and lifting it up on your shoulders. Every worry you pick up adds another brick, and every mile that you carry it adds to your level of weariness. Pretty soon your shoulders are aching, your back is breaking, and you are close to tears.

I know a much better way. Let me have those worries. I want to carry them for you. I want to take care of the problems that caused them. Bring them to me in prayer, and together we'll unpack them, one brick at a time. I want you to place each one in my hands and keep giving them back to me over and over until you get used to this fact: I'm here to lighten your load.

The Brick-bearer,
>God

== == ==   == == == == == == == == ==

THE PROBLEM IN THE UNIVERSE

Who can set me free from . . . this mortal body [of sin and death]? I thank God there is a way out through Jesus Christ our Lord.

Romans | 7:24–25 PHILLIPS

Dear One,

>A well-known English writer was asked by the *London Times* to contribute an essay on the topic "What is the problem in the universe?" His succinct reply was "I am."

This man understood a truth that applies to every person. A different job or husband or mother-in-law will fail to make a significant difference in your life. Having a better figure, a different bank balance, or more job benefits will not make you happy. Only when you face the places inside yourself that need my healing will things begin to change. Only when you stop quibbling about the externals and receive the deep, powerful love Christ died to give you will your life become all that I designed it to be.

Your Healer,
>God

== == ==   == == == == == == == == ==

HUMBLE YOURSELF

**Humble yourselves before the Lord,
and he will lift you up.**

| James | 4:10 |

Dearest Daughter,

>In a world that tells you to be the best, the fastest, the smartest, the richest, it might be hard to read the words "humble yourself." But believe me, they are words that can bring you peace. In situations where others are scrambling for the front of the line, I want you to quietly wait your turn. Even purposely let someone get in front of you, and pray for that person as you wait. If you find this hard to do, turn to me. Say, "Father, this is tough. Help me." And I will.

There's a tremendous payoff for the humble. To begin with, I'm crazy about humble people. (My Son was the humblest man who ever lived.) Here's another benefit: When you're humble, in my time and in my way, I will lift you up. Trust me.

Your Father,
>God

== == ==   == == == == == == == == ==

COLLECT YOUR INHERITANCE

I pray that you will begin to understand how incredibly great his power is to help those who believe him. It is that same mighty power that raised Christ from the dead and seated him in the place of honor at God's right hand in heaven.

Ephesians | 1:19-20 TLB

My Child,

>Suppose you received a call from a local attorney telling you to come in and pick up a check for one million dollars left to you by a wealthy relative. How long would it take you to get down to his office?

Well, you have a spiritual inheritance worth far more than a million dollars. It's my incredible power. My power can heal you when you're hurting, guide you when you're lost, and lead you through this challenging adventure called life. It is the exact same power that raised my Son from the grave—that's how strong it is. Yet at times you mope around like a spiritual pauper with nothing going for you at all. Come to me, my child, and collect your inheritance.

Your Wealthy Relative,
>God

== == ==   == == == == == == == == ==

NO SUBSTITUTE FOR ME

So he looked, and behold, the bush was burning with fire, but the bush was not consumed.

Exodus 3:2 NKJV

My Daughter,

>Someone once said that sin fascinates and then it assassinates. Sin draws the unwary person to its warmth and color like a campfire on a winter night. A campfire is beautiful, but if it's not kept in check, it can create a fire hazard and injure the ones who came to it for warmth.

I'm the God who can build a fire in your heart that brings warmth and light and meaning without burning you. When life is cold and lonely, seek the safety of my warmth and not the alluring, destructive fire of sin.

Your Warmth and Light and Meaning,
>God

== == ==   == == == == == == == == ==

A CHILD OF LIGHT

Ye are all the children of light, and the children of the day: we are not of the night, nor of darkness.

| 1 Thessalonians | 5:5 KJV |

My Daughter,

>I am totally light—no darkness at all. And since I live my life in you, you are a child of the light. So should you see your world as a place of shadows? Should you see your work as drudgery, your life as dull, your problems as impossible? Should you operate out of fear and hopelessness? Of course not.

The child of light inherits from me my character, my nature, my world view. She sees her work as an exciting challenge, her life as an adventure, her problems as faith-builders. She operates not out of fear, but out of faith; not out of hopelessness, but out of hope. In every situation, I want you to choose the light, my child.

The Father of Light,
>God

== == ==   == == == == == == == == ==

YOUR MIND IS LIKE A COMPUTER

As [a woman] thinketh . . . so is [she].

| Proverbs | 23:7 KJV |

My Daughter,

>Your mind is a lot like a computer. It believes the data you feed into it. If you feed it truth, it believes. If you feed it lies, it believes. And it not only believes, it implements that information into every program it runs so that the information becomes a part of how you act and decide.

This is why it's so important for you to choose to feed your mind the truth of my gospel every day. Feed in the data that I am your Father who loves and cares for you, that Jesus will never leave you nor forsake you, that the Holy Spirit will live within you and guide you. Memorize scripture. Listen to Christian tapes. Take notes during the sermon. Then watch those thoughts begin to change your life.

The Truth That Makes the Difference,
>God

== == ==   == == == == == == == == ==

CHANGE YOUR FOCUS

**I lift up my eyes to you, to you
whose throne is in heaven.**

| Psalm | 123:1 |

My Daughter,

>When you have a difficult assignment at hand, do you lower your head like a bull and go for it? Do you grit your teeth and bury yourself in the details of your objective?

I want to give you some advice. Don't lower your head; lift your eyes. Look to me. Commit your objective to me, whether it's a committee report or a decision to discipline a child. Look up and ask me to give you my perspective on what you're attempting. Ask me to give you my guidance and my game plan. Make sure that what you're doing doesn't conflict with my Word or my will. Then line up your plan of action and go for it.

The One to Whom You Look,
>God

== == ==   == == == == == == == == ==

GENTLE WORDS

If a Christian is overcome by some sin, you who are godly should gently and humbly help him back onto the right path, remembering that next time it might be one of you who is in the wrong.

| Galatians | 6:1 TLB |

My Dear Child,

>Once, Jesus came upon a mob of people. They were about to stone a woman who had been caught in adultery. He turned the mob away by saying, "Let the one who has never sinned cast the first stone." One by one the angry people slipped away. When he was alone with the woman, Jesus didn't yell at her or piously quote the Ten Commandments. Instead, with love in his eyes, he turned to her and gently said, "I do not accuse you. Now, you go and don't sin anymore."

My daughter, when you counsel with someone who has sinned, be sure to speak gently, without condemnation, as Jesus did. Remember, next time you may be the sinner in the scene.

The Lord of Mercy,
>God

== == ==   == == == == == == == == ==

ASK, SEEK, KNOCK

Ask and it will be given to you; seek and you will find; knock and the door will be opened to you. For everyone who asks receives; he who seeks finds; and to him who knocks, the door will be opened.

Matthew 7:7-8

My Daughter,

>If there were an agonizing question burning inside you, would you just sit around and never try to find the answer? If there were a key ingredient to your happiness hidden in a certain book, would you leave it on the shelf and never read it? If you knew the most meaningful gift you would ever receive lay on the other side of a locked door, would you just stare at the door and never knock on it? No, I'm pretty sure you'd ask the question, you'd read the book, and you'd knock on the door.

Come to me today. Ask whatever you want to ask. Seek whatever you long to know. Knock and gain admission to my presence. I'm waiting to meet you at the point of your need.

The One Who Answers,
>God

== == ==   == == == == == == == == ==

DON'T TOUGH IT OUT

There are friends who pretend to be friends, but
there is a friend who sticks closer than a brother.

Proverbs | **18:24 RSV**

My Child,

>From the pioneer woman who endured a solitary life, to the female
corporate executive who clawed her way up through the ranks of a
male-dominated system, self-sufficient women are often viewed as
heroes. But I didn't create you to exist in a vacuum. I created you to
need and enjoy other people. There's a place in you that will remain
empty and incomplete until you know the companionship of friends.

The best source of true friendships should be the body of Christ, the
family of my Son. And the best friend you'll ever have is Jesus himself.
So don't go it alone, my child. Reach out to others when you're lonely.
And grasp the hand of friendship when it's offered to you.

Your Friend and Father,
>God

== == ==   == == == == == == == == ==

DON'T WORRY! KEEP PRAYING!

Be happy in your faith at all times.
Never stop praying.

| 1 Thessalonians | 5:16-17 PHILLIPS |

My Daughter,

>When I ask you to be happy all the time and never stop praying, does that seem a little unreasonable? Wouldn't a person have to have a lobotomy before she could go around all day, every day, with a big smile on her face and a prayer mantra streaming from her lips? That's not what I'm talking about.

I know there will be happy times and sad times in your life, but there is a way to find happiness even in the midst of sadness. It comes from trusting that a loving God is in control.

And what about unceasing prayer? I'm not talking about praying aloud. Silent prayer can be as constant and natural as breathing. Silently pray for the people and events all around you. Silently pray for the needs my Spirit puts on your heart.

Be happy and keep praying,
>God

A DEEP WELL OF PEACE

**May the Lord of peace himself give you
his peace no matter what happens.**

| 2 Thessalonians | 3:16 TLB |

My Daughter,

>Have you ever known anyone who could just walk into a room and produce a spirit of peace? Even in the middle of personal conflict and confusion, that person just seems to carry with her an inner well of peace that affects everyone around her.

I want you to be that person in the situations and relationships of your life. How is it possible? Am I asking you to have a personality transplant? Yes, in a way I am. I'm asking you to let me put the personality of Jesus, the Prince of Peace, within you. I'm asking you to let me deposit in you such a deep well of the spiritual peace that emanates from him that you will be able to draw from it in every situation.

The Peace-giver,
>God

== == ==   == == == == == == == == ==

MY ROBE IS READY

He arose and came to his father. But while he was yet at
a distance, his father saw him and had compassion, and ran
and embraced him and kissed him. . . . The father said to
his servants, "Bring quickly the best robe, and put it on him;
and put a ring on his hand, and shoes on his feet."

Luke · 15:20, 22 RSV

My Daughter,

>I will never give up on you. You may turn away, but I never will.
Instead, I'll watch for your return. I'll wait at the window with my
running shoes on, ready to run out and welcome you. And when you
finally do come home, I won't make you grovel in my presence,
begging to be a servant in my house. I'll take you in. I'll throw a party
in your honor and celebrate.

You will always be my daughter, in spite of any wrong choices you
have made. My love is the robe that covers you. My grace is the ring I
place on your finger. My acceptance is the door that will always be
open for your return.

Your Father,
>God

== == ==   == == == == == == == == ==

COME TO ME EMPTY

**He has satisfied the hungry hearts and
sent the rich away with empty hands.**

Luke 1:53 TLB

My Daughter,

>If you try to pour water into a bucket that's already full, you'll end up spilling the water all over the ground. There are so many blessings I want to pour into you—the joy of an intimate relationship with me, the wonder of true worship, the adventure of facing new challenges with faith. I designed you to contain all of my gifts through my Holy Spirit.

But it's hard for me to pour anything into you when you come to me so full of other things—other worries and concerns, other people and possessions and passions. Set aside everything that concerns you, my child. Come to me empty so that I can fill you with my Spirit, my blessings, and my life.

The Life-giver,
>God

== == ==   == == == == == == == == ==

ENJOY YOUR LIFE!

**I have come that they may have life, and
that they may have it more abundantly.**

| | John | 10:10 NKJV | | | |

My Child,

>Enjoy your life today—the sights, sounds, and colors, the people,
prayer, work, music, and food. Jesus himself lived life to the full. He
enjoyed the companionship and hospitality of his friends. He rejoiced
in the beauty of my creation. And he found fulfillment in his
relationship with me.

Jesus came to earth so you could have a full and fulfilling life, not a
timid, half-hearted one—a joyful life, not a grim, dreary life that
settles for less than it can be. I want you to have a gracious, giving,
generous life of love that shares its gifts and blessings, not one that
holds back and hoards. So take advantage of the gift Jesus came to
bring you. This is your life. Celebrate each moment!

The Father of Life,
>God

== == ==   == == == == == == == == ==

DON'T MISS THE BEST PART

Jesus answered and said to her, "Martha, Martha, you are worried and troubled about many things. But one thing is needed, and Mary has chosen that good part, which will not be taken away from her."

| Luke | 10:41–42 NKJV |

My Dear Daughter,

>Each of my children has been given gifts. Martha's gift of hospitality was highly prized by those who received it. Mary's gift of listening with love made her delightful to know. Jesus valued both sisters. He never told Martha that her gift was worthless. What he did say was that all of Martha's bustling around serving others was robbing her of "the best part"—the eternal treasure of slowing down and hearing her Savior.

Where are you today? Are you using your gift as an excuse to stay too busy to hear my Son? Jesus appreciates all you've got to do. He also values your gifts. But more than anything, he wants you at his feet, hearing his heart, whether you are a Mary or a Martha. Draw near to him.

The Gift-giver,
>God

== == ==   == == == == == == == == ==

AT THE TOMB

We were therefore buried with him through baptism into death in order that, just as Christ was raised from the dead through the glory of the Father, we too may live a new life.

| Romans | 6:4 |

My Child,

>When you come to my Son, lay down your old life at the tomb. If you don't let it die, how can Jesus resurrect it? How can he give you a new identity if your old one is still alive and kicking? How can he set your wrong priorities right if you still have them clutched in your hand?

Whatever you refuse to bring to the tomb hasn't died, and it still has a stake in your life. It will hold you back and keep you struggling. If you want to be a new creation, you're going to have to lay everything down next to Jesus through prayer and repentance. Let the old man die with my Son through his sacrifice. Then embrace the amazing new life he will pour out in you.

Your Redeemer,
>God

== == ==   == == == == == == == == ==

LOVE YOUR IN-LAWS

So [Naomi] kissed [her daughters-in-law], and they lifted
up their voices and wept. And they said to her,
"Surely we will return with you to your people."

Ruth 1:9–10 NKJV

My Dear Daughter,

>When you marry, you become part of an extended family. Your
husband's parents become your parents. Likewise, when your
children marry, their mates become your children. Whether you find
them easy or difficult to love, your choice to love them will affect many
generations to come.

Look at the chain of events I brought from Naomi's loving relationship
with her Moabite daughter-in-law, Ruth. After Ruth's husband's death,
she followed Naomi to Israel. There she married Boaz and had a son
named Obed, who became the grandfather of King David. And it was
from David's line that Jesus himself was born. Naomi's choice to
embrace and care for Ruth and Ruth's choice to lovingly honor her
mother-in-law ultimately provided a family for my Son. My daughter,
let me use your love for your in-laws to bless your family.

The Lord of Families,
>God

== == ==   == == == == == == == == ==

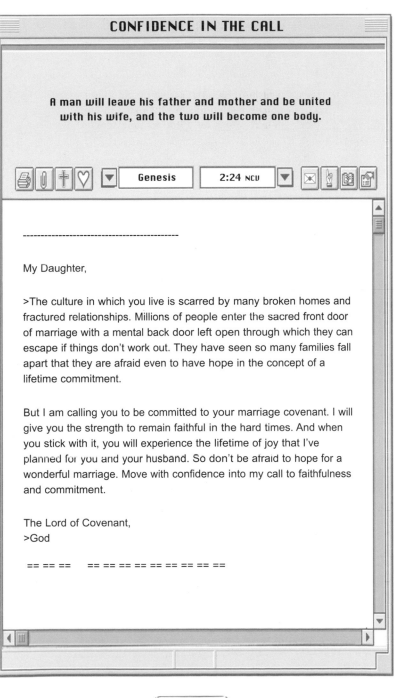

CONFIDENCE IN THE CALL

A man will leave his father and mother and be united with his wife, and the two will become one body.

Genesis   2:24 NCV

My Daughter,

>The culture in which you live is scarred by many broken homes and fractured relationships. Millions of people enter the sacred front door of marriage with a mental back door left open through which they can escape if things don't work out. They have seen so many families fall apart that they are afraid even to have hope in the concept of a lifetime commitment.

But I am calling you to be committed to your marriage covenant. I will give you the strength to remain faithful in the hard times. And when you stick with it, you will experience the lifetime of joy that I've planned for you and your husband. So don't be afraid to hope for a wonderful marriage. Move with confidence into my call to faithfulness and commitment.

The Lord of Covenant,
>God

== == ==   == == == == == == == == ==

FORGIVE THE WORST; HOPE FOR THE BEST

Do everything in love.

1 Corinthians | 16:14 NCV

Precious Child,

>Love is not for the hasty heart. It is not for the flighty, the frivolous, the faithless, or the fickle. Love requires a steadiness that does not give up or give in. It means bearing with your loved one's flaws while celebrating his gifts. It requires forgiving the worst while hoping for the best. Real love decorates the days with simple acts of kindness, small but thoughtful deeds that lift the spirit and light the dark corners of the soul.

Are you wondering if you have what it takes to love like this? I hate to tell you this, but apart from me, you'll find it impossible. But if you will turn to me, I'll fill you with the Spirit of love, through whom all things are possible.

The One Who Is Love,
>God

== == ==   == == == == == == == == ==

A HOUSE OF LOVE

**Everyone who hears my words and obeys them is like
a wise man who built his house on rock. It rained hard,
the floods came, and the winds blew and hit that house.
But it did not fall, because it was built on rock.**

Matthew   7:24-25 NCV

Beloved Daughter,

>How is building your family like building a house? In building a
house, you start with a strong foundation. Next, you raise walls of
protection. You add windows to let in light and fresh air, and doors to
allow people to come and go. And, finally, you put on a roof for
protection from the elements.

I want you to build your family on the unshakable foundation of my
Son, Jesus Christ. He will raise walls of security and love and open
windows of light that let in the wind of my Spirit. He is the door of
hospitality and compassion that will make your house a home. And he
is the covering you will need in the rough weather of life. Building a
strong and loving family is possible when you build on the Rock.

The Master Builder,
>God

== == ==   == == == == == == == == ==

LOVE SPEAKS SOFTLY

I may speak in different languages of people
or even angels. But if I do not have love,
I am only a noisy bell or a crashing symbal.

1 Corinthians **13:1 NCV**

My Daughter,

>Have you heard the voice of love? Love speaks softly, gently, sometimes even silently. Love will not get into a shouting match with the arrogant voices of a noisy world. It moves quietly through the day, meeting needs without a lot of fanfare. Love creates a climate where people of all ages feel safe to speak. It slows down to hear a child's question, an elderly person's stories, a teenager's frustration, a lover's sigh. Love says in a million caring ways, "You matter to me." It also says without any kind of sermon, "God loves you, and so do I."

So, my child, as you go through this busy day, speak in the language that every heart can hear. Speak love.

The Lord of Love,
>God

== == ==   == == == == == == == == ==

THE GIFT OF A HOME

**Open your homes to each other, without complaining.
Each of you has received a gift to use to serve others.
Be good servants of God's various gifts of grace.**

| 1 Peter | 4:9-10 NCV |

My Daughter,

>If you have four walls, a roof, and a front door where guests may enter, don't take it for granted. In a world where many are homeless and hungry, a home is a precious treasure, meant to be shared. It can be a castle or a cabin, an elaborate townhouse or a tiny apartment. However large or small, however elegant or plain, if you call it home, it is a gift. And if those within your walls love each other and love me, your home can be a tiny outpost of Heaven in a reckless world.

When you want to ask people in, make your guest list prayerfully. Don't invite only those friends with whom you feel comfortable. Include some who need ministry and some who need friends. Then throw open your doors and watch me work.

Your Guest at the Table,
>God

== == ==   == == == == == == == == ==

NO SPIRITUAL SIDE SHOWS

I may give away everything I have, and
I may even give my body as an offering to be
burned. But I gain nothing if I do not have love.

1 Corinthians 13:3 NCV

My Dear Child,

>I'm not calling you to be a Christian daredevil, putting on a big show
of holy stunts. I'm not expecting you to put on a spiritual sideshow for
this thrill-seeking world. What I want to see in you is the quiet, inner
conversion of your heart that will turn you from a self-seeker into a
God-seeker, from a self-lover into an other-lover.

The conversion of your heart won't make headlines. But, believe me,
it will be a miracle that will revolutionize your whole life. And once
your heart has been turned inside out by love, you'll find yourself
doing great things without even caring about the attention they bring.

The Heart-changer,
>God

== == ==   == == == == == == == == ==

MILE BY MILE

If you go the wrong way—to the right or to
the left—you will hear a voice behind you saying,
"This is the right way. You should go this way."

| Isaiah | 30:21 NCV |

My Dear Daughter,

>Walking with me is a long journey, so don't expect to arrive the first day. Take it mile by mile. Some days the road is smooth, and you make progress. Other days the road is full of rocks and ruts, and the going is rough. It's so easy to get discouraged on the rough days. It's tempting to turn back or quit. But don't give up. Instead, let me guide you.

Come to me each morning before you set out. Spread out your map, and we'll look at it together. I'll help you chart your course. And as you walk, I'll be right there with you, saying, "Turn left here, my child," or "Right at the next corner." Trust me on this journey of faith.

Your Guide,
>God

== == ==   == == == == == == == == ==

SET YOUR LIFE IN ORDER

Do all you can to live a peaceful life.
Take care of your own business, and do
your own work as we have already told you.

1 Thessalonians 4:11 NCV

My Daughter,

>Disorder and procrastination are twin "diseases" that rob you of
serenity. The cure to disorder lies in clearing out and simplifying. The
cure to procrastination lies in learning to deal with things as they arise
rather than letting them stack up.

If you'll straighten up and take care of business, you'll be surprised at
the inner sense of calm and confidence you'll discover. It will spill over
into every part of your life. You honor me when you create a peaceful,
orderly existence, for that peace is an advertisement for me in your
life. It draws others to you. Then you can lead them to me, and there
will be that many more peaceful hearts in this world of confusion.

The One Who Creates Order out of Chaos,
>God

== == ==   == == == == == == == == ==

PEACE IN THE UNPREDICTABLE

It has not yet been revealed what we shall be.

| 1 John | 3:2 NKJV |

My Daughter,

>There are people in your world who make a living predicting the outcome of future events. The weatherman comes on television several times a day to advise viewers as to whether they will need a sweater or an umbrella. Sports commentators predict winners in everything from football to horse racing. Stock market analysts predict market trends for eager investors. Everyone seems to want advance notice as to what will happen before it happens.

But the only certainty in your world is uncertainty. And the only peace in the midst of that uncertainty is placing your faith in me. Your decision to abandon yourself to my care in the midst of life's uncertainty is a decision to embrace life as a journey of faith and to experience each day as an adventure of spontaneous joy. Trust me, my child.

Your Certainty,
>God

== == ==   == == == == == == == == ==

EXPECT PERFECTION

**Our knowledge and our ability to prophesy
are not perfect. But when perfection comes,
the things that are not perfect will end.**

1 Corinthians   13:9–10 NCV

My Precious Daughter,

>Though you know you live in an imperfect world inhabited by
imperfect people, you can't seem to quiet that yearning within you for
a perfect life. That's because I placed that yearning in you. You see,
you were actually designed for perfection. The ache at the core of
your being is an unconscious memory of a place called Eden where,
for a moment in time, love and life were perfect.

Eden is gone now, but don't worry. As you pass through this imperfect
world, you are moving steadily toward perfect love and a perfect life
where every tear will be dried and the yearning in your heart will be
fulfilled. So forgive yourself and others when love falls short. And
content yourself with the hope of Heaven. It's going to be perfect.

Your Father,
>God

== == ==   == == == == == == == == ==

HOLD ON TO ME

**[Love] always trusts, always hopes, and
always remains strong. Love never ends.**

1 Corinthians 13:7-8 NCV

My Daughter,

>May your love be courageous. May it span your seasons of sorrow
and joy and flow through the ups and downs of life like a stream
through a rocky pass. In the hard times, may it reach to the depths of
your trouble, carving a channel through the bedrock of each problem,
bringing refreshment and hope. Over all the challenges and changes,
may love's courage persevere.

May you pour yourself out for others more and more until the stream
of love becomes a river, and the channel through which it flows grows
deep and sure and wide. If you allow my love to flow through you,
these things will come to pass as together we send love flowing out
into a hurting world.

The River of Love,
>God

== == ==   == == == == == == == == ==

YOUR HOME—A SANCTUARY

Do not change yourselves to be like the people of this world, but be changed within by a new way of thinking. Then you will be able to decide what God wants for you; you will know what is good and pleasing to him and what is perfect.

	Romans	12:2 NCV	

My Daughter,

>Though you are surrounded by the morals of a corrupt world, your home can be a sanctuary of grace and peace. Determine to create for yourself and your loved ones an atmosphere of hope and harmony where people are valued, friendships are nurtured, and my name is honored.

Fill your home with the blessings of life—flowers blooming, children laughing, a table spread with good things to eat. Make it a refuge, a safe place, where it's okay to be real and acceptable to admit weakness—a place where prayer binds up the raveled edges of each day's disappointments. In your home, may my words be welcomed and may my Son be your ever-present guest.

Your Father and His,
>God

== == ==   == == == == == == == == ==

MY LOVE FREES YOU

**Where God's love is, there is no fear,
because God's perfect love drives out fear.**

1 John   4:18 NCV

My Dear Daughter,

>There's no way to live fully, freely, and fearfully at the same time. It's just not possible. Freedom and fear cannot coexist. Fear's objective is to crash the party of your heart's joyful moment and imprison your heart in a cage of "what ifs." "What if this happens? What if that happens?" Fear can actually paralyze your faith when you need it most.

So call on me when you see fear's face at the door of your joy. My perfect love will drive fear far from you. Then, like a bird out of a cage, your heart will be released to soar, joyful in the knowledge that all of your "what ifs" are rendered powerless in the presence of my freedom.

The Love That Overcomes Fear,
>God

== == ==   == == == == == == == == ==

GET OUT OF THE GAME

Wait and trust the Lord. Don't be upset when others get rich or when someone else's plans succeed.

| | | Psalm | | 37:7 NCV | | |

My Child,

>Does it ever seem to you that the world is engrossed in a game called "MORE"? It's a scramble for more possessions, more money, more power, more prestige, more trophies. Personal worth is measured by numbers in the bankbook and cars in the garage. Watch out! This mentality is very seductive. It calls to you from magazine ads, TV commercials, and maybe even from the lifestyle of your next-door neighbors.

But my words to you are "wait" and "trust." Don't compare yourself with others. Get out of the game. Your worth has nothing to do with stuff and money. You are my priceless creation redeemed by my perfect Son. Find your identity only in me.

The One Who Loves You Perfectly,
>God

== == ==   == == == == == == == == ==

BE A CHRIST CONTAINER

I may have the gift of prophecy. I may understand all the secret things of God and have all knowledge, and I may have faith so great I can move mountains. But even with all these things, if I do not have love, then I am nothing.

1 Corinthians   13:2 NCV

My Daughter,

>The woman who is most like my Son is not necessarily the one who is the most gifted. Though Jesus was very gifted, the real hallmark of his character was love. Behind every awesome deed, motivating every amazing miracle, was a heart of love. Jesus was love incarnate, walking out my will in his daily circumstances.

To live as a Christian (a Christ-one) is to become a container filled with his Spirit of love. Giftedness counts for little if there is no love behind it. But once you are operating on Spirit power, the love of Jesus will motivate all you do. It will fuel your gifts and empower your faith. So come be filled, and live in love.

Your Loving Father,
>God

== == ==   == == == == == == == == ==

ACCEPT MY ACCEPTANCE

As soon as Jesus was baptized, he came up out of the water.
Then heaven opened, and he saw God's Spirit coming down
on him like a dove. And a voice from heaven said, "This is
my Son, whom I love, and I am very pleased with him."

Matthew   **3:16–17 NCV**

My Child,

>On the day of my Son's baptism, I looked at him and saw a man
waiting to honor me by fulfilling his destiny. I was bowled over with
love for him, and in front of the crowd gathered at the river, I said,
"This is my Son. I love him, and I am very pleased with him!"

I want you to know that every person alive is on a search for
significance, and everyone hungers to hear those words of
affirmation. I want you to hear them from me right now—today. You
are my daughter. I love you. I see that your heart's desire is to honor
me and fulfill your destiny, and I am very pleased with you. Come, live
in the reality of my acceptance.

Your Father,
>God

== == ==   == == == == == == == == ==

THROW CAUTION TO THE WIND

Then Mary took a pound of very costly oil of spikenard, anointed the feet of Jesus, and wiped his feet with her hair. And the house was filled with the fragrance of the oil.

| | John | 12:3 NKJV | |

My Daughter,

>Mary was criticized for wasting a costly jar of oil to anoint the feet of my Son. Her self-righteous critics said she should have sold the oil and spent the money on the poor. But Mary was willing to appear foolish or even wicked in order to pour out her greatest possession for her highest love.

Mary's extravagant love for Jesus contains a powerful lesson for you. In your relationship with my Son, don't hold back. Don't be so practical that you miss the joy of pouring out the best of yourself and your gifts for him and his kingdom. Others may advise caution. But I urge you to throw caution to the wind and love him with all your heart.

Your Extravagant Father,
>God

== == ==   == == == == == == == == ==

LET GO OF YOUR CRUTCH

**The . . . lame came to him at the temple,
and he healed them.**

| Matthew | 21:14 |

My Daughter,

>When you come to me crippled by life, I'm always willing to heal
you. But first you've got to be willing to put down your crutch. Putting
down your crutch will take faith, since you've probably been leaning
on it for quite a while. But how can I teach you to walk if you won't let
go. It will only get in your way if you insist on clinging to it.

What is your crutch? Your education, your addiction, your looks, your
friends, your job, your social standing? It could even be your religion.
You've got to let go of whatever you're leaning on, other than me, if
you ever want to walk in the Spirit. Come to me totally powerless, my
child, and I'll have you walking in no time.

Your Healer,
>God

== == ==   == == == == == == == == ==

WAKE UP TO THE CELEBRATION

I will sing to the Lord as long as I live. I will praise God to my last breath! May he be pleased by all these thoughts about him, for he is the source of all my joy.

Psalm 104:33-34 TLB

My Daughter,

>Don't lose your awareness of the mystery of life or the beauty of being alive. I know that it can be so tempting to just fall into the rut of checking things off your daily list and going to bed, only to wake up the next day and start all over. There is so much you're missing.

If you have fallen asleep to what's all around you, it's time to let me wake you up to this celebration called life. I place beautiful things on your way to work. Open your eyes to see them. I put unique people in your life every day. Notice them. Most importantly, I have given you a will to choose the wonder of daily living over the despair of daily dying. Choose the wonder.

The Source of Your Joy,
>God

== == ==   == == == == == == == == ==

LAUGH, DANCE, AND CELEBRATE!

**In Your presence is fullness of joy; in
Your right hand there are pleasures forever.**

Psalm   16:11 NASB

My Daughter,

>I didn't create you to walk around in sackcloth and ashes, wearing a
constant frown. I set you free for freedom. Yes, there is a time for
weeping and repentance, but it isn't all the time. Give it a rest!

If you feel that your joy has been sacrificed to a religious idol of false
piety, I say, let my joy start a celebration in your heart. Laugh out
loud. Dance as King David did. Sing with the angels. In my presence
there is true joy that fills the heart. The pleasure of my company is
not temporary. It is ongoing and everlasting. Don't wait till you get to
Heaven to start celebrating. Start here and now.

Your Joyful Father,
>God

== == ==   == == == == == == == == ==

THE BRIDEGROOM IS COMING

At midnight there was a shout, "Behold, the bridegroom! Come out to meet him."

Matthew 25:6

My Daughter,

>Many Christians have given up on the church. They believe in me, but they are down on what they call "the hypocrisy of organized religion." I don't want you to fall into this spiritual sinkhole.

The Church is the bride of Christ, and Jesus is the Bridegroom who's coming back for a beautiful, perfected bride. She is not perfect yet. But she is still the one betrothed to Jesus. And every Christian is called to beautify his bride as we await his coming. So, don't give up on the church. Jesus is not coming back for a scattered group of spiritual know-it-alls who mock his bride. He's coming back for a unified group of people who choose to accept the church's imperfections as their responsibility—a group of people who are committed to perfecting her.

The Bridegroom is coming,
>God

== == ==   == == == == == == == == ==

LET ME RENAME YOU

**You will be called by a new name which
the mouth of the LORD will designate.**

Isaiah 62:2 NASB

My Daughter,

>Many times girls grow up with fathers who speak curses over them rather than blessings. These girls will go into adulthood haunted by names like "Clumsy," "Stupid," or "Crybaby." I am your loving Father. If your earthly father labeled you with harmful names, I want to change your name.

If you have ever believed that your name was "Worthless," or "Insignificant," or "Black Sheep," I want your new name to be "Priceless in My Sight," "Awesome Child of the Father," "Eternally Loved and Accepted." With me in your life, you don't have to be haunted and driven by the old negative names. I want to change not only your name, but your destiny.

The One Who Knows You Best,
>God

== == ==   == == == == == == == == ==

DON'T DROWN IN YOUR BATHTUB

**All have sinned and fall short
of the glory of God.**

| | | Romans | | 3:23 | | | | |

My Daughter,

>Do you know that it is just as possible to drown in your own bathtub as it is to drown in the Pacific Ocean? When a self-righteous woman secretly looks down on a woman who is drowning in an ocean of obvious and public sin, that self-righteous woman is actually drowning in a bathtub of subtle self-righteousness.

Every person is imperfect and sinful. It doesn't matter whether he drowns a hundred miles down as a murderer or an inch below the surface as a gossip. Only through Jesus' going down to the depths and being raised up above the surface can anyone be saved. So if you're tempted to judge others, remember that my grace is the only thing powerful enough to keep your head above water.

Your Lifeguard,
>God

== == ==   == == == == == == == == ==

LIVE A LIFE THAT STRETCHES YOU

**With men it is impossible, but not with God;
for with God all things are possible.**

Mark   10:27 KJV

My Daughter,

>I have great things planned for you, but it's going to involve taking some chances. If you always play it safe, you will never experience the miracle of my work in you. If you are always swimming in pools where you're an arm's length from the edge, you won't experience the thrill of pushing past your limits.

I don't want you to live a reckless life, but I do want you to live a life that stretches you. Follow me beyond your own personal strengths and abilities to a place where the wonderful things that happen in your life can only be explained by my presence in you. Don't limit yourself to what you do easily and comfortably. Live life beyond your boundaries.

The Father of Limitless Possibilities,
>God

== == ==   == == == == == == == == ==

THE EYE OF THE STORM

Be still, and know that I am God. I am exalted among the nations, I am exalted in the earth!

| | Psalm | 46:10 | | | | | |

My Daughter,

>Life runs at such a frantic pace. If people are forced to wait in line for more than a minute, they think, *Why is this taking so long?* Instant gratification is the mantra of the modern world.

Sadly, it is also becoming a mantra chanted in the church. Some people want a spiritual drive-up window attached to my house. But a hurried existence kills the spirit. I want you to seek stillness and calmness as most people seek wealth.

To be still and calm in the midst of a busy world is to adopt a counter-cultural lifestyle. It is choosing to be the eye at the center of life's hurricane. Sit and focus on me. You will find the clarity to see the lie of the fast and furious. Come. Take time to know me, to hear me, to become who I want you to be.

Your Peace,
>God

== == ==   == == == == == == == == ==

WHAT MOVES YOU?

**If you love me, you will obey
what I command.**

John   14:15

My Daughter,

>Just as the tides of the ocean are drawn by the moon, just as the
clouds are blown by the wind, you will be moved by something. Some
people are moved by fear. Some are moved by a need to impress
others. People who obey me because they fear hell or because they
want to appear holy to others don't really get to know me or my love.

I want you to be moved by love alone. Love is the force at the center
of my being, and until you allow that reality to move you, your motives
will be mixed at best. So come to me. Read my Word. Enter the two-
way conversation known as prayer. As you get to know me, you'll be
drawn by the power of my love into a life of obedience.

The Heartbeat of Love,
>God

== == ==   == == == == == == == == ==

OPEN YOUR MAIL

How sweet are your words to my taste, sweeter
than honey to my mouth! . . . The unfolding of your
words gives light; it gives understanding to the simple.

| | Psalm | 119:103,130 | |

My Daughter,

>Suppose you went to your mailbox and found a letter from your best
friend. Would you store it on a bookshelf without reading it? Would
you display it on a coffee table without ever breaking the seal and
finding out what it had to say? I don't think so! You'd rip into it and
read every word your friend had written.

Do you believe that I am the best friend you'll ever have? I am. And
I've sent you a letter called the Bible. It reveals intimate clues to my
character. It contains advice and comfort and a vision for your future.
Please, don't just leave it out on display or file it on a shelf. Crack into
the good news and read. You're gonna love this book!

Your Father and Friend,
>God

== == ==   == == == == == == == == ==

REFERENCES

Scripture quotations marked AMP are taken from *The Amplified Bible, Old Testament.* Copyright © 1965, 1987 by Zondervan Corporation, Grand Rapids, Michigan. Used by permission.

Scripture quotations marked NCV are taken from *The Holy Bible, New Century Version,* copyright © 1987, 1988, 1991 by Word Publishing, Dallas, Texas 75039. Used by permission.

Scripture quotations marked KJV are taken from the *King James Version* of the Bible.

Verses marked TLB are taken from *The Living Bible,* copyright © 1971. Used by permission of Tyndale House Publishers, Inc., Wheaton, Illinois 60189. All rights reserved.

Verses marked THE MESSAGE are taken from *The Message,* copyright © by Eugene H. Peterson, 1993, 1994, 1995. Used by permission of NavPress Publishing Group.

Scripture quotations marked NASB are taken from the *New American Standard Bible.* Copyright © The Lockman Foundation 1960, 1962, 1963, 1968, 1971, 1972, 1973, 1975, 1977, 1995. Used by permission.

Scripture quotations marked NKJV are taken from *The New King James Version.* Copyright © 1979, 1980, 1982, Thomas Nelson, Inc.

Scripture quotations marked PHILLIPS are taken from the *New Testament in Modern English,* (Rev. Ed.) by J. B. Phillips. Copyright © 1958, 1960, 1972 by J. B. Phillips. Reprinted by permission of Macmillan Publishing Co., New York, New York.

Scripture quotations marked RSV are taken from *The Revised Standard Version Bible,* copyright © 1952 by the Division of Christian Education of the Churches of Christ in the United States of America and is used by permission.

ABOUT THE AUTHOR

An award-winning lyricist, popular writer, and sought-after speaker, Claire Cloninger is one of the country's foremost Christian communicators. She is a five-time Gospel Music Association Dove Award winner whose Christian songs have been widely recorded by such artists as Amy Grant, Sandi Patti, Wayne Watson, and B. J. Thomas. She has written more than two dozen musicals for church choir including *My Utmost for His Highest, Experiencing God,* and *Welcome to Our World.*

Claire's inspirational books include *E-Mail from God for Teens, More E-Mail from God for Teens, A Place Called Simplicity, Simple Joys, When the Glass Slipper Doesn't Fit,* and *Postcards from Heaven.*

Claire holds a B. A. and an M. A. in Education from the University of Southwestern Louisiana in Lafayette, where she was named Outstanding Alumna in 1991. Her teaching skills are put to good use in her national ministry as an inspirational speaker and retreat leader.

Claire and her husband, Robert, an artist, reside in a log home on the banks of a river in Alabama. They are active members of Christ Anglican Church, where he is Chairman of the Evangelism Committee and she serves on the Parish Prayer Team. They are the parents of two grown sons and grandparents of two granddaughters and one grandson.

If you have enjoyed this book, or if it has
impacted your life, we would like to hear from you.
Please contact us at:

RiverOak Publishing
Department E
P.O. Box 700143
Tulsa, Oklahoma 74170-0143

Additional copies of this book
and other titles in the *E-mail from God* series
are available from your local bookstore.

E-mail from God for Teens
More E-mail from God for Teens
E-mail from God for Men
E-mail from God for Kids
E-mail from God for Teens screensaver

RIVER
OAK
PUBLISHING